The Institute of Chartered Financial Analysts Continuing Education Series

Understanding Securitized Investments and Their Use in Portfolio Management

October 23, 1990
New York, New York

Michael J. BeVier
Allan G. Bortel, CFA
Owen Carney
James V. Dillon
Kenneth B. Dunn
Juan M. Ocampo

Helen Frame Peters
Scott F. Richard
Dexter Senft
William J. Welsh
Jerald M. Wigdortz

Edited by
Ken M. Eades
Diana R. Harrington
Robert S. Harris

Sponsored by the
Association for Investment
Management and Research

Additional copies of this publication may be ordered from:

Association for Investment Management and Research
P.O. Box 7947
Charlottesville, VA 22906
1-804-977-5724 (Phone)
1-804-977-0350 (Fax)

The Association for Investment Management and Research comprises the Institute of Chartered Financial Analysts and the Financial Analysts Federation.

Katrina F. Sherrerd, CFA, *Managing Editor*
Joni L. Tomal, *Associate Editor*
Charlene Semer, *Associate Editor*
Nina D. Hutchinson, *Typesetting/Layout*

ISBN 1-879087-07-3

Printed in the United States of America

3/27/91

Table of Contents

Foreword vii

Biographies of Speakers ix

Overview of the Seminar 1
  Ken M. Eades, Diana R. Harrington, and Robert S. Harris

Value Added or Complex Gimmick? 6
  Michael J. BeVier

The Development of the Securitized Market 14
  Helen Frame Peters

Valuation Challenges: Mortgage-Backed Securities and CMOs 20
  Scott F. Richard

Strategies for Using Securitized Assets in Managing Pension Portfolios 31
  Kenneth B. Dunn

Valuation Challenges: Asset-Backed Securities 40
  James V. Dillon

The Application of Securitization on Corporate Balance Sheets 46
  Jerald M. Wigdortz

Securitization and Strategic Planning for Banks and Thrifts 50
  Juan M. Ocampo

Understanding Securitization in Analyzing Common Stock Investments, Part I 57
  William J. Welsh

Understanding Securitization in Analyzing Common Stock Investments, Part II 61
  Allan G. Bortel, CFA

The Effects of Securitization on Bank Regulation in the 1990s 66
  Owen Carney

The Future of Securitization 71
  Dexter Senft

Self-Evaluation Examination
  Questions 76
  Answers 80

Foreword

Securitization is the process of pooling and repackaging assets into securities that can then be traded in financial markets. In a relatively short period of time, securitization has come to play an increasingly important role within the major domestic capital markets around the world. Many people in the industry believe that it will have a major impact on the structure and operation of financial markets and institutions, particularly the banks and thrifts. Others feel that significant barriers will constrain that growth.

The term "asset-backed securities market" describes any financial structure in which future cash flows from a pool of loans or receivables serve as the primary collateral for new securities issues. The most-developed sector of the present asset-backed market is mortgage-backed securities. Credit card receivables, automobile loans, leases, and other non-mortgage assets have also been securitized. Not all types of collateral are equally attractive candidates for securitization, however. Furthermore, many types of asset-backed securities are complicated and carry significant risks, not all of which are easy to discern. Valuation, for example, requires the use of powerful theoretical and empirical models.

Although securitization is growing rapidly, the sources of information about it are few. This sparsity of literature on the subject motivated AIMR's seminar, "Understanding Securitized Investments and Their Use in Portfolio Management," held in New York on October 23, 1990. This seminar addressed a wide range of issues relating to securitization, including the development of the securitization market, valuation challenges, strategies for using securitized assets in managing pension portfolios, strategies for using securitization in banks and thrifts, and the valuation implications of securitization on financial statements.

AIMR wishes to extend its sincere appreciation to the outstanding group of experts who served as seminar speakers and assisted in the publication of these proceedings: Michael J. BeVier, MorBanc Financial Corporation; Alan G. Bortel, CFA, Sutro & Co., Inc.; Owen Carney, Office of the Comptroller of the Currency; James V. Dillon, Security Pacific National Bank; Kenneth B. Dunn, Miller, Anderson & Sherrerd; Juan M. Ocampo, McKinsey & Company; Helen Frame Peters, UBS Securities; Scott F. Richard, Goldman, Sachs & Co.; Dexter Senft, The First Boston Company; William J. Welsh, J.P. Morgan Investment Management, Inc.; and Jerald M. Wigdortz, Salomon Brothers Inc.

We are also indebted to Ken M. Eades, Diana R. Harrington, and Robert S. Harris of the University of Virginia for their assistance in editing this publication and for their helpful insights into the subject.

Thanks also go to several individuals who contributed to the development of the seminar: James R. Vertin, CFA, Chairman of the AIMR Education Steering Committee; Michael J. BeVier; Diana R. Harrington; Robert S. Harris; and Susan D. Martin, CFA, Vice President of AIMR, who organized the seminar.

We hope you will find this publication a valuable addition to your library.

Katrina F. Sherrerd, CFA
Vice President
Research and Publications
AIMR

Biographies of Speakers

Michael J. BeVier is Co-Founder of the MorBanc Companies and serves as Chief Executive Officer of the principal funding facilities operated by MorBanc: MorBanc Mortgage Company, L.P., MorBanc Capital Corporation, and Mortgage Bankers Financial Corporation. Prior to founding MorBanc, he owned Michael J. BeVier Associates, Inc., a consulting firm specializing in mortgage securities. Mr. BeVier was closely involved in the design and creation of the California Housing Finance Agency, including much of the political negotiations surrounding passage of the enabling legislation which he describes in his book, *Politics Backstage*. A member of the State Bar of California and the American Bar Association, he has also served as a consultant to the FHA Commissioner in Washington, D.C. Mr. BeVier holds a B.A. from Carleton College, a J.D. from Stanford Law School, and an M.B.A. from the Stanford Graduate School of Business.

Allan G. Bortel, CFA, is Vice President and a member of the specialized Depository Institutions Financing & Advisory Group within Sutro & Co.'s Corporate Finance Department. Prior to joining Sutro in 1990, Mr. Bortel was a senior vice president in the Equity Research Department of Shearson Lehman Brothers. He was previously a securities analyst and director of research for several California-based stock brokerage firms and was assistant to the president of the Federal Home Loan Bank of San Francisco. Since 1973, Mr. Bortel has been listed among the top five analysts covering the savings and loan field in *Institutional Investor* magazine's annual poll of money managers. He earned a B.S. degree at The Wharton School of the University of Pennsylvania, attended the London School of Economics, and received an M.B.A. in finance from University of California at Berkeley.

James V. Dillon is a Vice President with the Interest Rate and Currency Risk Management Group of Security Pacific National Bank. Within this department he is a member of the Financial Institutions Group, which is responsible for advising banks, insurance companies, money managers, and other financial institutions on the use of swaps, caps, and swaptions to manage their interest rate and currency risk. His prior experience includes work in mortgage-backed securities and commercial real estate finance. Mr. Dillon earned an M.B.A. in finance from Columbia University and an undergraduate engineering degree from Manhattan College, and recently completed a post-graduate program at New York University focused on the capital markets.

Kenneth B. Dunn is a Partner and Fixed Income Portfolio Manager with Miller, Anderson & Sherrerd. Prior to joining the firm in 1987, he was a professor of finance and economics at Carnegie-Mellon University. An author of articles in leading financial journals, Dr. Dunn was the first to develop a model for the valuation of mortgage securities that explicitly modeled uncertainty and the homeowner's prepayment option. He holds a B.S. and M.B.A. from Ohio State University and a Ph.D. from Purdue University.

Juan M. Ocampo is a Principal at McKinsey & Company, Inc., where he concentrates on corporate strategy advice for financial institution clients. He has served a number of investment banking, commercial banking, and thrift clients in the areas of strategies, organization, and profit improvement. He is the co-author of *Securitization of Credit*. Mr. Ocampo holds a B.S. in economics from the Massachusetts Institute of Technology and an M.B.A. from Harvard University.

Helen Frame Peters is a Managing Director of UBS Securities Inc., with responsibilities for the Mortgage Finance, Asset-Backed Finance, and Financial Institutions Advisory Groups. Ms. Peters joined UBS Securities in 1988 after serving as president of Security Pacific Financial Strategies, Inc., and managing director of Security Pacific Merchant Bank. Her prior experience includes vice president and group manager of the debt strategy group, member of the fixed income management committee, and vice president of mortgage-backed research at Merrill Lynch; assistant vice president at Philadelphia Saving Fund Society; and manager of the research department at the Federal Reserve Bank of Philadelphia. She holds a B.A. in economics, an M.A. in statistics, and a Ph.D. in finance from The Wharton

School of the University of Pennsylvania.

Scott F. Richard is Vice President of Fixed Income Research and co-head of the Research and Model Development Group at Goldman, Sachs & Co. His responsibilities include the development of analytical prepayment and valuation models for mortgage-backed securities and related derivative products and the development of mortgage-related new products. Before joining Goldman Sachs, Dr. Richard was a professor of financial economics at Carnegie-Mellon University. Additionally, he served as an associate editor of both the *Journal of Finance* and the *Journal of Financial Economics* and has published numerous articles in scholarly journals on a wide range of financial subjects. Dr. Richard holds a B.S. in electrical engineering and sciences from the Massachusetts Institute of Technology and a D.B.A. from Harvard University.

Dexter Senft is a Managing Director of The First Boston Corporation and head of their Fixed Income Research Department. In his 16 years at First Boston, his responsibilities have also included product development, structured finance, and technology planning. Mr. Senft created several of the modern analytical concepts and tools in the mortgage market and has published many articles on these subjects. He has been described as the "father" of the CMO, having structured the first such deal in June 1983. Mr. Senft has served as a member of the board of advisors of the *Journal of Portfolio Management* and the Mortgage Education Committee of the Public Securities Association. Mr. Senft is a graduate of Rice University with degrees in mathematics, mathematical sciences, and economics.

William J. Welsh is Vice President of Equity Research at J.P. Morgan Investment Management, Inc., where he follows the banking securities and investment management industries. Prior to joining J.P. Morgan in 1986, he was the bank analyst at Sanford C. Bernstein & Co. His previous experience also includes positions at Westinghouse Electric Corporation and Resource Planning Associates. Mr. Welsh earned a B.S. in engineering from the University of Pennsylvania and an M.B.A. from Harvard University.

Jerald M. Wigdortz is a Managing Director of Salomon Brothers Inc, where he is responsible for asset securitization, including consumer receivable securitization, CMO arbitrage and structured finance, commercial mortgage securitization, U.S. government asset sales, and quantitative support. Mr. Wigdortz joined Salomon Brothers in 1973 and worked at Salomon Brothers International Limited from 1974 to 1980, where he ran the firm's Eurodollar CD trading operation. He returned to the New York office and was named manager of money market sales, trading, and finance in 1983. Mr. Wigdortz earned a B.S. in physics from Stevens Institute of Technology and M.S. and M.B.A. degrees from the University of Michigan.

Overview of the Seminar

Ken M. Eades
Associate Professor of Business Administration

Diana R. Harrington
Professor of Business Administration

Robert S. Harris
Professor of Business Administration

Colgate Darden Graduate School of Business Administration
University of Virginia

Securitization is the process of pooling and repackaging loans (or other receivables) into securities that can then be traded in financial markets. Relatively new to financial markets, this process began with the introduction of mortgage-backed securities in the early 1970s, courtesy of the Government National Mortgage Association (Ginnie Mae). Despite a relatively short history, securitization has already had widespread effects on our financial system, yet the process and its effects remain a mystery to many investors and policymakers. This publication comprises presentations by experts in the field of securitization. They offer the reader a basic understanding of securitized investments, as well as important insights into the role of securitized products in portfolio management, the effects of securitization on financial intermediaries, the resulting implications for analyzing investments in intermediaries, and the potential future developments in securitized markets both in the United States and abroad.

The Basic Process of Securitization

Securitization has changed the shape of financial markets. For most of modern history, financial intermediaries have played the essential role of channeling funds from net savers to net borrowers. Such a conduit for funds ultimately increases the ability of the economy to make real investments and reap their rewards. For years, the dominant form of intermediary was the bank (or bank-like savings institution), which gathered funds from thousands of individuals and loaned out such funds to thousands of borrowers.

To illustrate the basics of securitization, consider the savings and loan (S&L) industry, which traditionally specialized in mortgage lending. The stylized S&L's assets were a portfolio of individual mortgages, and its liabilities were thousands of individual deposit accounts. Through the intermediation process, the S&L pooled risks by holding many mortgages, bridged maturity needs between borrowers and lenders, and economized on information and monitoring costs (because individual savers did not have to assess the risks of individual mortgage loans). In this traditional intermediation, the individual mortgages were themselves not marketable assets, given the possibilities for prepayment and the unique credit risk of each homeowner.

The securitization process in essence makes these mortgages marketable by creating packages of mortgages that provide the underlying cash flow for traded mortgage-backed securities. These traded securities are simply claims on the cash flow from the mortgages. Given prepayment and credit risk, the cash flow from any given mortgage is not easily predictable, but reasonable forecasts of flows across a mortgage pool are possible for a large diversified set of mortgages with certain demographic characteristics.

Securitization, in fact, can change the very nature of some financial intermediaries. Because the mortgages can now be sold with securitization, the traditional S&L no longer has to hold mortgage assets; rather, it can originate loans that are then securitized and sold. Nor does the originator have to service the loan. Anyone who has had a home mortgage in recent years is probably well aware of the many parties involved in the loan. Securitization uncouples the traditional roles of origination, ownership, and servicing, once performed mainly by savings institutions.

Why didn't securitization happen earlier? To pool and keep track of large loan pools and their cash flows requires the ability to monitor and process large amounts of information. To a large extent, then, securitization is possible because of the rapid improvements in computer and communications technology.

This simplest form of mortgage-backed securitization allows mortgages to be bought directly by a wider array of investors, broadening the supply of mortgage funds. Just as a corporation obtains lower-cost funding by issuing debt into the market (as opposed to borrowing from an intermediary), the securitization process opens the mortgage market to new participants.

Challenges and Questions

Securitization has gone far beyond this simplest form as financial engineers have entered the picture. Cash flows from mortgage pools are carved into increasingly complex contracts (tranches), which differ in maturity and risk characteristics. Other types of assets, including credit card debt and automobile loans, also have been securitized. As a result, portfolio managers are presented with a seemingly ever-expanding array of opportunities to purchase securitized products. At the same time, analysts and regulators face the challenge of understanding the nature and implications of these products in a rapidly changing financial sector. For example:

1. What will the cash flow on the asset (mortgage) pool be, and what is it worth? The answers to these questions depend on detailed models of the individual cash flows (including credit risk and payment schedules) as well as the prevailing rates of return on other assets (such as government bonds).
2. In what ways can the cash flow on the asset pool be divided to appeal to a larger class of investors? Some claims may be essentially risk free, having first claim on cash, while other claims may have more uncertain payments, depending on such factors as mortgage prepayment or default rates.
3. How does securitization affect financial intermediaries and the analysis of intermediaries in a securitized world? For instance, the securitization of mortgages has led to a more plentiful supply of mortgage funds, which has reduced the cost of mortgage money (relative to government borrowing costs). The lower mortgage rates compress the spread that is essential for profitability

for many intermediaries. Some go so far as to point to securitization as a major reason for the decline of the S&L industry.
4. What types of assets can be securitized, and what is the future of securitization? To date, credit cards, automobile loans, and other assets have been securitized, but other forms of loans, such as middle-market corporate lending, remain unsecuritized. As of 1991, securitization has spread to some economies outside the United States; will it be a global phenomenon?
5. In what ways can securitized investment products be useful to portfolio managers? Securitized products, especially those in which cash flows have been divided into many classes, provide almost limitless cash flow profiles for a portfolio manager. Yet, their very complexity may lead the unwary astray.

The presentations in these proceedings address these and many additional demanding questions.

Value and Structure of Securitization Technology

In "Value-Added or Complex Gimmick?" Mike BeVier provides a provocative look at whether securitization increases the efficiency of our financial system or whether it is merely a complex gimmick that generates fees for some but does little, if anything, to create value for our economic system. BeVier notes that securitization allows investment managers to make their own risk assessments of specific assets rather than relying on the judgments of bank managers. This securitization process provides major economic benefits to our system and a more efficient distribution of risks across investors. Although many financial intermediaries are weakened by securitization, BeVier points to the narrowing of the spread between mortgage and U.S. Treasury rates as evidence of the benefits of securitization in the mortgage markets.

BeVier goes on to discuss some of the complex details of securitization products that often include numerous tranches with arcane acronyms. He notes that such tailored securities can be highly valuable in asset/liability management. The complexity of the products also allows for manipulation of accounting data or tax liabilities. He concludes that securitization adds value but that successful users of these products must be sure to invest in the information and skills necessary to understand these complex products.

In "The Development of the Securitized Market,"

Helen Frame Peters discusses the evolution of securitization in the United States. She pays particular attention to the structure of asset-backed securities and some of the key features an investor or chief financial officer must consider in looking at them.

From an issuer's perspective, Peters notes advantages of securitization, including lower funding cost, improved financial position, increased market share, better timing of income, and improved asset/liability management. The securitization process also creates many operational challenges, however. The issuer must examine the scheduled cash flows from the underlying loans or receivables, screen assets for their suitability as collateral, and structure the asset-backed security properly. The structure must ensure that the credit of the asset pool is separated from the credit of the issuing institution. This separation, which requires careful attention, is essential if the investor in securitized assets is to be protected in event the institution files for bankruptcy subsequent to securitizing assets. Peters discusses the details of structuring, including the role of credit enhancement.

Understanding Securitized Assets and Their Use

The "valuation challenges" section of this volume contains presentations by Scott Richard, James Dillon, and Kenneth Dunn. These speakers bring to light the concepts and terminology that investment analysts, pension fund managers, and arbitragers use to assess the value and risks of asset-backed securities. Dunn and Richard restrict their comments to mortgage-backed securities and their derivatives, collateralized mortgage obligations (CMOs). Dillon examines some of the more recent securitized assets, including credit card receivables and automobile loans.

The crux of Scott Richard's presentation, "Mortgage-Backed Securities and CMOs," is that mortgage-backed securities and their derivatives are too complex to value without powerful theoretical and empirical models. Mortgage-backed securities are difficult to value because of the difficulty of estimating the interest rate risk, credit risk, and risk of mortgages prepaying. By comparison, the valuation of a CMO is inherently more difficult because each tranche represents a slice of the total risk/return spectrum embodied in a mortgage-backed security.

Interest rates and the path that interest rates follow over time are particularly important determinants of the cash flows received by investors in mortgage-backed securities and CMOs. If interest rates happen to fall over a given period of time, a larger number of mortgages will be prepaid than if rates had

risen during the period. In fact, a unique cash flow stream is associated with every possible path that interest rates could follow over the time period. Richard argues that adequately capturing the complexities associated with valuing mortgage-backed securities requires a simulation model.

Richard's simulation model is driven by an arbitrage-free model of the term structure of interest rates. Each interest rate path scenario generated by the term structure model is associated with an estimate of the level of prepayments, as well as an estimate of the new refinancing rate. The prepayment risk is what distinguishes mortgage-backed securities from other, more conventional securities.

The interest rate simulation provides a theoretical rationale for why mortgages are prepaid, but a significant number of prepayments cannot be predicted on the basis of an interest rate theory alone. For example, *seasoning* and *monthly* prepayment effects are related more to the reasons homeowners sell their houses than to the level of interest rates. Thus, Richard concludes that prepayment rates are best estimated using empirical models. These prepayment rate estimates are then fed into the term structure model to generate the option-adjusted spread (OAS). The OAS is the additional yield over the simulated Treasury rates that equates the simulation value with the market price of the mortgage-backed security.

In "Strategies for Using Derivative Mortgage-Backed Securities in Pension Portfolios," Kenneth Dunn presents his insights about the relation between the mortgage-backed securities and CMO markets. He observes that CMOs are less liquid than their underlying mortgage-backed securities and that they are inherently more difficult to value because of the reallocation of the risk/return structure of the mortgage-backed securities within a CMO deal. The valuation difficulty is in determining how sensitive the CMO's market value is to interest rate changes and how it is positioned in the prepayment and default risk spectrums. In this regard, Dunn echoes BeVier's concern that the complex structure of a CMO has arisen less because of investors' demands than because of the suppliers' desire to *hide the ball*—that is, to obscure how the risk is reapportioned among the many tranches of the deal. Despite the valuation difficulties, however, a CMO has the advantage that it can be structured to look more like, and therefore compete more directly with, corporate and Treasury bonds.

Dunn focuses his comments on how fund managers can use CMOs effectively to manage the risk/return characteristics of their portfolios. For example, he observes that the negative convexity inherent in a portfolio of mortgage-backed securities may be offset by adding principal-only strips to the portfolio. Thus, a pension fund manager can alter the fund's payoff patterns in any number of ways by adding the CMO having the necessary piece of a mortgage-backed security's risk/return spectrum. Dunn warns, however, that no amount of financial engineering is prudent unless the securities being added to the portfolio are fairly priced.

The standard tools of risk and return measurement, duration, and OAS must be applied carefully to a CMO tranche. For example, Dunn argues that a 100-basis-point OAS should be interpreted very differently for adjustable-rate and 30-year fixed-rate mortgages. To highlight how misleading OAS can be, Dunn shows how the prepayment assumptions used to value a particular CMO tranche led to an estimated OAS of 1900 basis points and an average life of only 0.42 years.

In "Asset-Backed Securities," James Dillon discusses the more recent developments in securitization and how interest rate swaps can transform these new securities into more desirable ones. In particular, he discusses how a synthetic floating-rate security can be created by combining an asset-backed security with an interest rate swap. He argues that asset-backed securities are better suited for this sort of financial engineering than mortgage-backed securities because of more predictable cash flows, shorter average life, and higher relative yields. To emphasize the viability of this arbitrage strategy, Dillon provides historical evidence illustrating that swap spreads have exceeded credit card and automobile receivable spreads over Treasuries.

Costs and Benefits of Securitization

In "The Application of Securitization on Corporate Balance Sheets," Jerald Wigdortz deals with the benefits and costs of securitization to investment-grade and to noninvestment-grade companies. In both cases, securitization can produce direct cost reductions to the companies using this technology.

For investment-grade institutions, one benefit of securitization is well known: off-balance-sheet financing and its positive effect on financial institutions' capital ratios. Two other benefits also accrue to the investment-grade institution—increased tax efficiency, and insulation against event risk. Tax benefits of securitizing assets can accrue to those corporations having either excess foreign tax credits or interest credits on U.S. debt allocated to foreign operations. Securitization also insulates the issuer from event risk, a risk that was real and expensive in the late 1980s.

Wigdortz suggests that the advantages for noninvestment-grade companies are less well known and

have not yet been tapped to any extent. First, companies can use such assets as receivables, mortgages, franchise payments, or cash flows from other high-quality assets—divisions, for example—to create off-balance-sheet securitized financings. The assets, he suggests, may carry creditworthiness greater than that of the corporation that holds the securitized assets. For example, he suggests that the credit quality of accounts receivable depends on the creditworthiness of those owing money, not the firm holding the receivables. Wigdortz notes that hard assets—assets whose market value is well known or knowable—are easier to consider securitizing. In addition to asset-backed securitization, companies may also use this technology for restructuring debt such as bridge loans from banks, senior subordinated debt, PIKs, or other exotic securities not already directly tied to assets.

In "Securitization and Strategic Planning for Banks and Thrifts," Juan Ocampo, taking the point of view of banks and thrift institutions, discusses the attractiveness of various assets and the operational and environmental risks. He suggests that real estate-backed securities do not have as predictable loss patterns or as stable collateral as the ideal asset for securitization. He considers credit card and accounts receivable portfolios that are well managed to be superior for securitizing. The key for Ocampo is good management, monitoring, and credit analysis. Ocampo adds one benefit of securitization to the list that Wigdortz provides—he suggests that financial institutions that securitize are forced to examine many of their activities with greater care (for instance, their market segment).

Analyzing Common Stocks of Companies that Securitize

William Welsh, in "Understanding Securitization in Analyzing Common Stock Investments," addresses the impact of securitization on corporate financial statements, and the difficulty that the changes create for stock analysts. Welsh provides a primer on the concerns that a stock analyst must have in reading and interpreting a financial statement for a company that securitizes. Indeed, he contends that the analyst must understand that analysts' traditional focus on asset size, growth, and financial performance is obsolete. As an example of the changes that can occur in financial statements, Welsh describes how Citicorp reports securitized credit card income as noninterest income rather than net interest income. If analysts did not know this, they could think that credit card assets have not grown during the past two years, even though they have grown steadily.

Welsh suggests that securitization does entail risks, some of which are not easy to discern. One type, rebound risk, is real and must be the concern for equity analysts. Rebound risk is the residual credit exposure the issuing institution retains from a securitized portfolio. This type of risk would include, for example, capped losses on securitized assets and price limit guarantees of repurchase. Rebound risk is difficult to measure but is nonetheless important to the potential stock investor. Other risks analysts must examine result from adverse selection or excessive complexity of the instruments.

In "Understanding Securitization in Analyzing Common Stock Investments," Allan Bortel discusses the impact that securitization has had on the profitability of the thrift industry. He also describes the role Fannie Mae and Freddie Mac play in the securitization process and expresses concern about probable government support if these agencies find themselves in trouble. In a somewhat different way, he reflects the theme of many of the speakers: This is a new world, part of which we do not understand, and the future effects of which are as yet unpredictable.

Future of Securitization: Regulation, Products, and Countries

Owen Carney reports on "The Effects of Securitization on Bank Regulation in the 1990s" and the issues facing the Comptroller of the Currency. Carney notes that securitization still involves loan origination, servicing, credit enhancement, underwriting, and other traditional banking activities. Currently, the Comptroller's office is focusing on four key areas: (1) ac-counting, (2) risk-based capital; (3) new powers for banks, and (4) investment limitations. Carney provides a thoughtful discussion on each, with specific comments on the Comptroller's current thinking. A key factor in discussing securitization is the extent to which a bank that sells assets (securitizes them) has any future liability on those securitized assets. The Comptroller wants to establish procedures such that when a bank sells assets without any recourse, no recourse exists from that point forward.

Dexter Senft discusses "The Future of Securitization." He notes that many claims about the expansion of securitization to new products and other countries are much too optimistic and fail to take into account some of the basic difficulties and constraints in the securitization process. For instance, he cites two prime constraints to expanding securitization around the globe: (1) lack of depth and breadth in most countries' financial markets, and (2) lack of desire or need to sell assets. Senft also comments on the future of securities backed by nonmortgage assets such as credit card debt. Senft does not believe these securities will become as complex as those that have developed in the mortgage markets, for which the average number of tranches per deal had reached 11.3 by 1990. This prediction follows from a discussion of underlying factors, including the smaller amount of risk in many asset-backed securities (compared with mortgage-backed securities) and the reluctance of issuers to lend their names to complicated deals. Despite these cautions about the pace of development in securitization, Senft sees the number of issues continuing to increase. From a product development standpoint, however, Senft sees no fundamental innovations in the near future for asset-backed securities.

Value-Added or Complex Gimmick?

Michael J. BeVier
Chairman
MorBanc Financial Corporation

Does securitization add value by increasing the efficiency of financial markets, or is it merely a gimmick whose principal effect is to provide employment for investment bankers and facilitate the process of selling to unwitting clients?

I believe that securitization can create real value by bypassing expensive intermediation and providing securities structured to meet the needs of specific investors. The resulting increase in complexity, however, creates the potential for abuse. Securitization, therefore, places new demands on investors to have specialized skills and knowledge.

Intermediation Versus Transparency

Traditionally, investment managers have relied on intermediaries to assess and capitalize lending risk. The intermediation process is illustrated in **Figure 1**, in which providers of funds—lenders, depositors, and creditors—are shown at the top, and borrowers are shown at the bottom. The intermediary is in the middle, receiving deposits and other investments and deciding where best to employ them. Investors analyze the weighted-average risk/return profile of the intermediary's current portfolio and decide whether its capital is sufficient to cover the risks incurred.

Intermediaries, such as banks, thrive on lack of information: You do not know the borrowers, but the bank does. Securitization reduces the need for intermediaries. As represented in **Figure 2**, securitization provides a more transparent structure through which investment managers can make their own risk assessments. The transparency of securitization greatly reduces the intermediaries' role, providing several major advantages.

First, transparency reduces uncertainty. Intermediaries are extremely difficult to analyze, as witness the miscalculations by sophisticated bank investors during the past year. These institutions possess a constantly changing portfolio of multiple assets on which good information may be unavailable or unreliable. They are often highly leveraged and subject to interest rate risk that cannot be easily measured. They are operating entities with the attendant risks of uncertain and certainly fallible management. Most intermediaries are subject to government regulation, the restrictions and demands of which are impossible to project. In contrast, an asset-backed security rests on a highly specific, usually static pool of cash flow assets that are isolated in a trust or bankruptcy-remote corporate structure. This greatly simplifies the task of risk measurement by reducing the uncertainty of that analysis. The reduction in uncertainty also reduces the risk premium required by investors.

Second, transparency reduces the direct costs of intermediation. To support their substantial overhead and to provide an adequate return on shareholder capital, intermediaries require a spread of 100 to 200 basis points on top of direct origination and servicing costs. Securitization is much less expensive. An underwriter's spread on asset-backed securities will usually amount to less than 25 basis points; legal, rating, and other costs add 15 to 20 basis points more. Even after the costs of credit enhancement are added by paying a surety or structuring a subordinated class, the costs are far less than those of direct intermediation.

Third, transparency permits more efficient distribution of risks. Investors can more accurately gauge whether a specific pool of assets offers the type of risk/return profile they seek. Furthermore, securitization accommodates explicit structuring of risk. For example, the asset originator might take a limited first-loss position. A subordinated class with intermediate risk characteristics might be sold to high-yield investors, and a surety might take catastrophic risk by backing the senior class that is sold to investors with very low risk/return preferences.

The Incidence of Added Value and the Effect on Banks

If securitization increases the efficiency of capital markets, who benefits? There is evidence of gains to both investors and borrowers. The benefit of mort-

Figure 1. The Traditional Intermediation Process

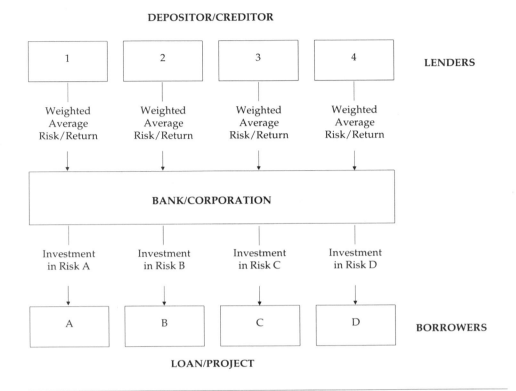

DEPOSITOR/CREDITOR

| 1 | 2 | 3 | 4 | LENDERS |

Weighted Average Risk/Return (×4)

BANK/CORPORATION

Investment in Risk A | Investment in Risk B | Investment in Risk C | Investment in Risk D

| A | B | C | D | BORROWERS |

LOAN/PROJECT

Source: MorBanc Financial Corporation

gage securitization to borrowers is suggested by Figures 3 and 4. **Figure 3** shows the percent of outstanding mortgage debt that is securitized (a rolling average from 1979 to 1989). **Figure 4** shows a rolling average spread of mortgage rates over Treasury rates. As the volume of mortgage securitization rose during this period, mortgage yield spread to Treasuries declined by about 30 basis points. On a $150,000 30-year home mortgage, this represents a before-tax saving to the homeowner of $450 per year.

Figure 5, which shows the spread of various AAA-rated securities over Treasuries, indicates the benefits of securitization to investors. The spreads on mortgaged-backed securities are option-adjusted; that is, the options component within the mortgage-backed security is removed to make it more comparable to a traditional corporate bond. Each of the asset-backed securities provides more yield than traditional corporate bonds. This suggests that some of the value resulting from securitization also flows to the providers of funds.

In short, the transparency of securitization increases the efficiency of capital flows. There is evidence that investors and the ultimate users of funds share these benefits. This is the good news. Two other aspects of securitization are more sobering, however.

First, securitization has severely weakened inter-mediaries and will continue to do so. **Figure 6** shows the amount of commercial paper outstanding, along with the total amount of mortgage-backed securities and asset-backed securities outstanding during the past 10 years. Compare this rise in securitization with **Figure 7**, which shows the composite rating of domestic bank holding companies over the same period. The inverse correlation is striking and not merely coincidental. It is being argued, I think persuasively, that securitization will destroy banking as we know it. This may be ultimately desirable, but in the short run, failure of major banking institutions, along with many smaller ones, will cause considerable discomfort in both the public and private sectors. This subject will require much thought, which I leave to others more expert in banking and regulatory policy.

A second concern is one that arises in shifting from a broad view of securitization's role in capital markets to the gritty complexities of structuring, valuing, and trading these instruments.

Efficiency Versus Gimmickry

Securitization of mortgages began in the early 1970s. Mortgage-backed securities have been around longer than any other type of asset-backed security and are

Figure 2. The Securitization Process

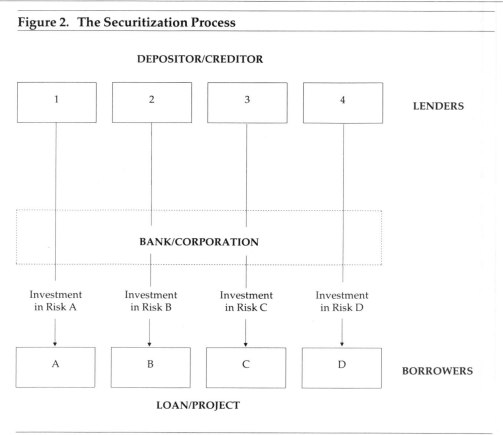

Source: MorBanc Financial Corporation

the most highly evolved form of securitization. **Exhibit 1** presents a partial list of different types of classes currently available from the multiclass mortgage-backed securities called collateralized mortgage obligations (CMOs). The number of different structures and their complexity is almost bewildering, even to those with years of experience in this industry. The question is whether such increasing complexity in securitized products furthers the real efficiencies of securitized intermediation or at some point becomes counterproductive.

The original idea behind multiclass CMOs was to package cash flows from a single pool of collateral into separate bond classes, each of which was structured to meet the preferences of different kinds of investors better. This seems sound. Some investors like long maturities, some like short. Some want highly stable cash flows, others are less concerned about shifts in duration. By specializing the cash flows, you may obtain real gains from trade.

The first CMO was sold in 1983, and through 1986, the types of CMOs created were fairly straightforward structures, usually with three sequential-pay classes paying current interest and one accruing Z-bond that paid out last. Most of those in Exhibit 1 have been created in the past three years.

Exhibit 2 lists some of the structural elements that these increasingly complex structures were designed to address. The very first CMOs appealed to investors with different term preferences. The first class, with an average life of two to three years, would be sold to a bank or thrift; the second, with a five- to seven-year life, to, say, an insurance company; and the third, with a 10- to 12-year life, to a bond fund. Z-bonds were often included because the accretion feature substantially increased the duration and appealed to investors with very long liabilities such as pension funds. Very short-duration LIBOR floaters were developed later to appeal to foreign investors, and this spawned the inverse floater, which provided a negative duration instrument for hedging purposes.

Credit risk was structured through senior/subordinated classes, which could include multiple subordinated classes with different priorities. These obviously appealed to investors with different risk preferences and degrees of mortgage credit expertise.

Perhaps the most influential development in the past three years has been the structuring of volatility with planned amortization classes (PACs). These are designed to minimize duration changes caused by fluctuations in prepayment rates on the underlying mortgage pool. The ability of mortgagors to prepay

Exhibit 1. Types of CMO Securities

ARB	Ascending rate	PIOW	PACIO w/wt. avg. cpn.	SPZ	Subordinate PCZ
F	Floater	PO	Principal only	STC	Subordinate TAC
I	Inverse floater	PPO	PAC PO	STF	Subordinate TCF
IO	Interest only	PLQ	PAC liquidity	STI	Sup. TAC inv. floater
IOW	IO w/wt. avg. cpn.	PSF	PAC SF	STR	Straddle
Jz	Jump-Z bond	R	Residual	STZ	Subordinate TCZ
LOV	Low volatility	RPC	PAC residual	SUF	Support floater
LPZ	Retail PAC Z	RS	Subsidiary residual	SUP	Support payer
LQ	Liquidity	RSP	Res. subsidized PAC	SZ	Support Z
OPZ	Optimal Z-bond	RTC	Reverse TAC	TAC	Targeted amount
PAC	Planned amort.	RTL	Retail	TCF	TAC floater
PACW	PAC w/wt. avg. cpn.	RTZ	Retail Z-bond	TCZ	TAC Z
PAY	Clean payer	SF	Super floater	TIO	TAC IO
PCF	PAC floater	SI	Support inv. floater	TPO	TAC PO
PCZ	PAC Z-bond	SJZ	Support jump-Z bond	TR	Total return bond
PCZW	PAC Z w/wt. avg. cpn.	SOC	Subordinate PAC	XAC	Indexed alloc.
PI	PAC inv. floater	SPF	Subordinate PCF	XPF	Ext. protect floater
PIO	PAC IO	SPI	Subordinate PIF	XPO	Subordinate PPO
PIOF	PAC IO floater	SPO	Super PO	XXX	Undefined
PIOI	PAC IO inf. floater	SPP	Super PAC PO	Z	Clean accrual

Source: "CMO Passport." ® Reprinted by permission of Merrill Lynch Mortgage Capital Inc. Copyright 1990.

their loans at any time is equivalent to their being long on a put option on the indebtedness. The short position is held by the mortgage investor. The greatly increased cash flow stability of the PACs largely insulates their holders from this options cost. PACs therefore appeal to a wider range of fixed-income investors who wish to avoid the event risk of corporate bonds but require assurance that they are not simply trading decreased credit exposure for greatly increased option risk.

Although the increasing variety and complexity of security structures has potentially increased inter-mediation efficiencies, it also has increased the possibilities for zero-sum trading. For example, the inclusion of PACs within a CMO requires the existence of "support" classes that absorb the volatility taken out of the PACs. Support classes may offer value to investors less concerned with volatility, but the complexity of these CMOs, which often have 15 to 25 classes, requires considerable expertise and attention to make accurate valuations. Structuring at times resembles a shell game not to match investors' needs but to hide the option risk from them.

The care required by CMO investors becomes evi-

Figure 3. Percent of Outstanding Mortgage Debt Securitized

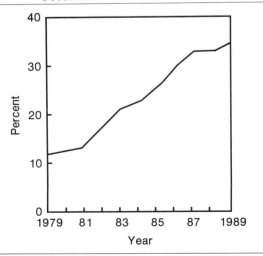

Source: Author; using data from *Federal Reserve Bulletin*, table "Mortgage Debt Outstanding." (December issues, 1979-89).

Figure 4. Mortgage Rates Spread over Treasury Rates

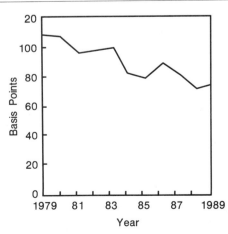

Source: Author; using data from *Federal Reserve Bulletin*, tables "Mortgage Markets" and "Interest Rates in Money and Capital Markets" (December issues, 1979-89).

Figure 5. Selected AAA-rated Bond Spread over Treasuries (In Basis Points)

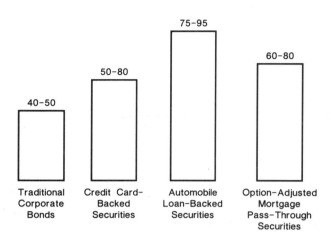

Source: MorBanc Financial Corporation

Figure 6. The Growth of Securitization Versus Commercial Paper (1980-90)

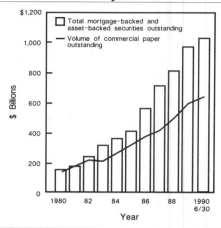

Source: Author; data compiled from "Asset-Backed Securities Quarterly Reference Guide," Fourth Quarter 1989-February 1990, Dean Witter Reynolds, Inc.; and *Federal Reserve Bulletin*, Table 1.54 (December issues, 1980-90).

dent in looking at **Figure 8**. This is a 13-class CMO issued in 1990 and currently traded. The diagram shows the changing pattern of cash flows under three different PSA assumptions. Note particularly the stability of PAC classes A and B over all three scenarios, compared with the wild fluctuation of support class E even with the rather mild change in prepayments from 75 percent to 160 percent PSA.

A final example of structural elements involves manipulation not of cash flows, but tax liability. Taxation of multiclass securities is extremely complex, especially for the holder of the "residual" class, which receives any spread that exists between the coupon on the underlying mortgage collateral and the coupons on the several classes of CMO bonds. Commonly, the taxable income in the early years of the CMO greatly exceeds the cash received, creating what is often termed "phantom income." In some cases, a CMO is structured so that the residual class receives almost no cash but is required to recognize substantial amounts of taxable income. In these cases, the

security is not an investment but merely a liability, and the issuer must pay someone to hold it.

These residual classes are subject to abuse. They are, for example, qualified investments for real estate investment trusts. Because real estate investment trusts report and distribute taxable income to their shareholders, purchase of CMO residuals with substantial amounts of phantom income results in overstatement of economic earnings. That portion of distributions attributable to phantom income is simply the shareholders' principal being returned to them in the guise of earnings. This result will reverse in later years when the residual throws off phantom losses,

Exhibit 2. Multiclass Securities: Elements and Structures

Structural Element	Example Structures
Term	Sequential Pay Classes
Duration	Z-Bonds/Floaters/Inverse Floaters
Credit Risk	Senior/Sub
Volatility	PACs/TACs
Tax exposure	Residuals

Source: Morbanc Financial Corporation

Figure 7. Change in Composite Rating of Bank Holding Companies (1980-90)

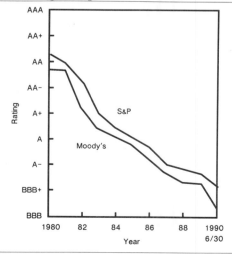

Source: *Historical Rating Perspective.* New York: Duff & Phelps/MCM Investment Research Co. (September 1990).

Figure 8. Cash Flow Volatility in CMOs with PAC Classes

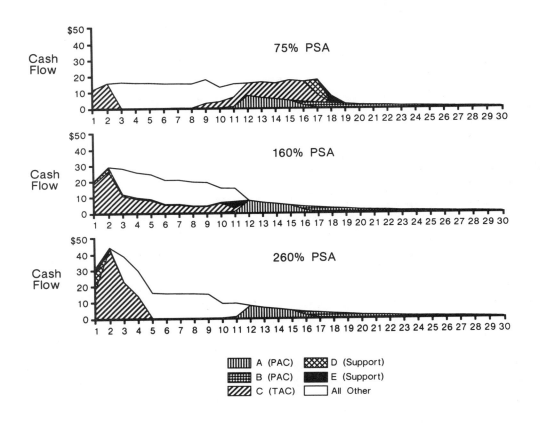

Source: MorBanc Financial Corporation

but the distortion of income in the early years can be very misleading.

Figure 9 compares the spread over Treasury rates of a pool of Government National Mortgage Association (Ginnie Mae) collateral with the weighted-average spread of the CMO backed by those Ginnie Maes. The pickup is 12 basis points, which may be an accurate measure of the value imparted to these cash flows by restructuring them into a multiclass CMO. A portion of that spread, however, may also represent no more than a successful trade by the issuer to one or more ignorant buyers.

Conclusion

Securitization represents a fundamental advance in the way capital is intermediated. It promises substantial increases in intermediative efficiencies by eliminating the need for expensive middlemen and facilitating the movement of capital throughout the world.

Securitization reduces costs by making capital transactions more transparent. A potential investor is able to see through an asset-backed security to the underlying collateral and make his own assessment of risk. Such securities may be further enhanced by breaking the underlying cash flows into multiple security classes that meet specific investment criteria.

Despite the promise of added value, this more direct interchange between investors and borrowers still has certain troubling aspects. Securitization is a principal reason for the failure of the thrifts and for the rapidly declining health of U.S. banks. The failure of legislatures to change banking regulations to accommodate the narrowing spreads and disintermediation caused by securitization will result in further bank failures and billions in losses for deposit insurance funds.

The process of securitization itself can be abused. The increasing complexity of securities has at times outstripped the ability or willingness of investors to value them properly. This permits the promise of increased efficiencies to be perverted into vehicles for

Figure 9. Structure of Multiclass Securities

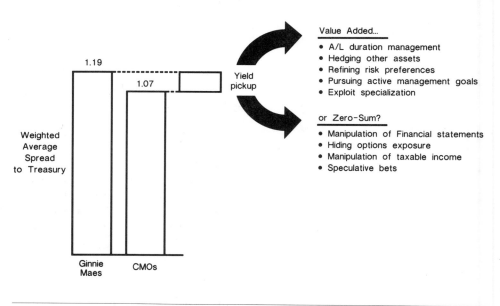

Source: MorBanc Financial Corporation

sharp trading or manipulation of financial statements.

Securitization is a powerful, but complex, tool. It bestows on investment managers a considerably larger role in the process of global capital allocation. To ensure that its considerable benefits are fully realized and to prevent abuse, managers must fully understand the intricacies of these instruments. They require greater knowledge and perhaps more specialization than other investments. Any failure in rising to this increased responsibility would not only demean the profession but also squander the opportunity for greater allocative efficiency of the world's capital resources.

Question and Answer Session

Question: What factors are affecting spreads, particularly the spreads on automobile- and credit card-backed issues in the market today?

BeVier: Spreads vary among asset types, but they also vary over time. Spreads on automobile-backed issues have fluctuated wildly this year. They were as low as 70 basis points several months ago, and as high as 110 basis points recently. The duration characteristics and the strength of the issuers were about the same, so the 40-basis-point difference results from changing supply and demand along with spread relationships that drive certain derivative trades. For example, many investors do LIBOR swaps against automobile loan securities. As loan swap spreads rise, so do spreads on automobile loan securities. The spreads are also related to differences in the assessment of risk among types of securities. For example, potential prepayments pose greater options risk in automobile-backed securities than in credit card-backed securities. The spreads certainly have reflected that difference.

Peters: Year-end balance sheet improvement mechanisms also generate increases in spreads. Right now most investors and most issuers are aware that this happens, so we almost anticipate it.

Question: Do you think it makes sense for a nontaxable institutional life insurance company to own CMO residuals?

BeVier: I think it makes sense for some organizations. Residuals can be exceptional investments if bought at the right price. Most people are afraid of them—and they should be—because residuals are so complicated. This provides real opportunities for those who can properly analyze them: You can find real value there.

Question: Do you think historical data are adequate guides for understanding the credit risks of securitized products?

BeVier: Historical analysis is extremely valuable, but not sufficient. It must be combined with a careful look at the originator's overall track record and underwriting procedures, as well as the quality of the servicing and collection procedures of the loan administrator. Many rely on the rating agencies to make these assessments because they look at underwriting and servicing procedures before issuing a rating. In some cases, however, you may wish to make an independent judgment.

Question: Please comment on the markets and the marketability of these securities in the United States and abroad.

BeVier: I believe we were among the first private issuers to have our bonds actively marketed in Europe, and we have sold some of our bonds in Asia, as well. Thus far the market abroad has been quite limited, but I believe this will change in the near future. Buying these securities right requires time and attention, but the yield pickup is there for those willing to take the trouble to learn. The additional yield and freedom from corporate event risk will become increasingly attractive to investors worldwide. Asset-backed securities will be common investments globally by the end of the decade.

Question: Do you see the securitized market growing rapidly in the next few years?

BeVier: Yes. I believe it will grow in several ways: volume, diversity of asset type, range of investor base, and liquidity. I think it represents a fundamental and permanent shift in the way capital is intermediated.

The Development of the Securitized Market

Helen Frame Peters
Managing Director
UBS Securities

It is difficult to untangle the components of today's financial markets. Values we thought were staid and true for many years are changing, and one of the biggest changes is in securitized markets. Securitization is the process of pooling and repackaging loans and other receivables into securities. Although it is a relatively new technology, securitization has become a mainstay of modern financial markets, but as yet it remains almost unheard of outside the financial community. Securitized markets play a major role in the financial system, but the word *securitization* is not even in the dictionary. Most who are aware of the securitization phenomenon, however, believe it will have a major impact on the structure and operation of the financial markets and could permanently alter financial institutions as we know them.

The continued evolution of the process of securitization will provide new investment opportunities for market participants as well as test the existing system of financial intermediation. As assets are more readily sold, financial institutions will cease to provide the intermediation function. As a result, some observers believe, financial institutions will become stronger as they are forced to compete in this changing market. Institutions will specialize in areas where they have a competitive advantage, such as origination, servicing, deposit generation, or custodial services. Others contend that a continuing rise in securitization will add to the already weakened position of the financial markets. Institutions that securitize the bulk of their assets will cease to benefit from asset diversification. Good assets will be securitized while bad assets remain on the books, and as a result, insurers, stockholders, regulators, and ultimately the American public will suffer as confidence in the financial system further erodes.

Key to an understanding of the current structure of the asset-backed securities market is a knowledge of the historical evolution of the market and its principal players. Of equal importance are the motives leading to securitization and some of the practical consequences for institutions issuing asset-backed securities. The origination, servicing, and structuring of asset-backed securities requires numerous choices with legal, tax, and accounting implications.

The Evolution of Securitization

Securitization began with the advent of the Government National Mortgage Association (Ginnie Mae) securities in the early 1970s. Ginnie Mae securities are collateralized by pools of Federal Housing Administration (FHA) and Veterans Administration (VA) single-family mortgages. They are backed by the full faith and credit of the U.S. government and are sold to a wide variety of institutional and retail investors. As the asset securitization market matures, a wide array of assets have been securitized, and credit enhancement structures other than the backing of the U.S. government have been readily accepted by investors.

Although a majority of asset-backed securities are still collateralized by single-family residential mortgages, other types of assets—credit cards, automobile loans, commercial multifamily loans, junk bonds, leases, boat loans, and various trade receivables—have been securitized by banks, thrifts, and financial institutions. By mid-1990, nearly $90 billion of non-mortgage assets had been securitized. Compared to the residential mortgage market, this is still a small amount. Today, nearly 40 percent of all single-family residential mortgages are securitized. The securitization of assets will continue to grow. By the end of the century it is expected that securitization of all asset classes will reach $1 trillion.

Before the advent of asset securitization, there were basically two forms of financing that corporations and municipalities could use to tap debt markets: loans, usually originated by banks, and corporate debt securities such as notes, bonds, and commercial paper. In each case, the ultimate investor—whether he lent money or bought securities—had to concern himself with the underlying credit of the corporation or issuing entity.

Securitization provides the end investor with the opportunity to look past the issuing entity to a collateral pool which, if structured properly, would provide the primary source for the payment of interest and the repayment of principal. As a result of securitization, corporations and other issuers can create debt structures that have expected return and risk characteristics that are totally unrelated to the issuer's inherent financial structure. A properly structured asset-backed transaction would enable an issuer to tap the capital markets at debt-rating levels significantly higher than its current corporate debt-level rating.

Investors are concerned with their exposure to risk of loss or delayed payment of the cash flows that they are entitled to receive under the terms of a security agreement. Traditional debt securities are subject to more of this risk than a properly structured asset-backed transaction. In traditional security structures, the bankruptcy of the issuer could severely jeopardize the amount and timing of the cash flows the investor ultimately receives. In asset-backed vehicles, the security is structured to be bankruptcy remote; that is, the bankruptcy or insolvency of the issuing organization will not interfere with the investor's receipt of designated cash flows from the security.

Properties of Asset-Backed Securities

All properly structured asset-backed securities have the following characteristics:

- Investors will receive principal and interest payments derived from the pooling of a group of loans or other receivables.
- The cash flow from these assets will be restructured or enhanced to improve the likelihood that the investor will receive the expected interest and principal payments.
- The bankruptcy or insolvency of the issuer will not affect the timely distribution of these specified cash flows from the asset pool.
- The offering will be in the form of a security rather than a loan or participation.
- The legal structure of the security will be set forth so as to meet the tax and accounting needs of the issuer and a targeted investor base.

Although all asset-backed securities have these basic similarities, they are not all alike. With the exception of government-guaranteed mortgage-backed securities, there is only rudimentary standardization in the asset-backed market. Asset-backed securities may differ in several key aspects: asset type, maturity, scheduled amortization features of the assets, cash

flow structures of the security, prepayment or repayment of the assets, servicing and processing procedures, quality of the underlying assets, and type and quality of the credit enhancement vehicles.

Because of the lack of standardization, investors need to analyze the features of asset-backed structures. The structural and perceived differences in risk, even among equivalently rated securities of the same asset type, can generate differences in market acceptance, liquidity, and, ultimately, market price. Over time, the asset market will mature and greater standardization will ensue, but in the interim a savvy investor and an astute CFO must remain up-to-date on the latest advances in this relatively new technology.

Motives for Securitization

From an issuer's perspective, there are many reasons why a corporation might choose to sell or pledge its receivables through an asset-backed issuance. Some benefits may be purely economic or financial in nature, but often the decision to securitize is in response to tax, legal, regulatory, accounting, or strategic considerations. One reason for issuing asset-backed securities is to lower funding costs. Asset-backed issues usually receive a higher credit rating and, thus, lower market cost than is otherwise attainable by the corporation. In addition, any restructuring of the asset's cash flow may have broadened the investor base and generated additional cost savings.

Improved financial position is another reason for issuing asset-backed securities. For example, regulatory requirements or rating agency and market leverage concerns may make it necessary or advantageous to sell certain assets. An appropriately structured securitization can achieve an asset sale that will improve capitalization ratios. In addition, if servicing is retained, the additional fee income will enhance a return on assets.

Increased market share is a third reason for issuing asset-backed securities. The periodic sale of assets can enable an institution to increase its originations, taking advantage of economies of scale that may be inherent to its origination or servicing process. Citibank, for example, has taken full advantage of this.

Income is another important consideration. By selling assets, an issuer can shift income from spread income to fee income, booked at the time of sale, and earned from servicing the assets over the life of the transaction.

Finally, an institution might use securitization to improve its asset liability management. Through securitization, assets can be removed from the balance sheet, thereby reducing the potential funding exposure inherent in the financing alternatives.

Securitization and the Operations of Issuers

Asset securitization is not without its costs for an issuing institution. For example, institutions must have adequate portfolio tracking systems and investor reporting systems in place. For many, this requirement may necessitate major overhauls of existing servicing systems. Systems that monitor the timely payment of principal and interest may be inadequate for valuation of assets or portfolio management. Many systems cannot segregate the asset pools to investors. Changes to major production systems may be costly and time consuming for all involved. System considerations should be addressed early by an issuer because they can affect the timing and feasibility of a transaction.

The process an institution goes through to prepare an asset-backed security provides insight into the fundamental worth of the asset. The process can be broken into three categories: portfolio analytics, pool selection, and servicing and structuring.

Portfolio Analytics

The assets that are targeted for securitization must be analyzed thoroughly to determine their potential value to the investor. Investors want to know both the structure of the asset's cash flows and the potential for future losses resulting from defaults and foreclosures. The individual assets are combined into a large pool, and thus the uncertainty of any one asset's default is replaced by estimates of expectations of the portfolio's default and delinquency rates. Historical statistics are generated for various subgroups of the asset pool and are analyzed carefully for insight into the future performance of the securities.

Many institutions have never taken a serious look at their portfolio of assets. To initiate an asset securitization, institutions must be able to provide breakdowns of the assets in their portfolio by coupon maturity, loan type, loan purpose, collateral, borrower characteristics, demographics, and any other loan or borrower characteristics indicative of relative value in the market. Those who have done due diligence in preparation for a securitization can attest that many times the loan files have not been previously reviewed. A review of the loans may show interest rates recorded at odd percentages, missing maturities, and many other problems. One must also review the prepayment or repayment patterns of these assets. Finally, in specialized cases, some of the data may have to be converted to investors' accounting methods, such as the conversions of Rule of 78 automobile loans to actuarial accrual methods.

Pool Selection Process

The pool selection process involves screening assets for their suitability as collateral. A system must be able to illuminate unacceptable assets and provide evaluation, ranking, and optimization of loans to be included in the structure. An optimal portfolio is generated from the potential pool. Once the security structure has been set, it must be integrated into the existing computer system. The system must have the capability to track any necessary advances that must be made to the servicer and to accommodate flows of funds from the credit enhancement vehicle. Finally, there are various ongoing needs such as:

- marking and recording assets to be sold to ensure the perfection of the investor's security interest;
- segregation of funds that are due the investor;
- daily identification of payments of principal or interest due investors;
- transference of payments to special accounts, if necessary;
- handling of reversals resulting from bad checks or other incorrect entries that may have been sent to investors but must be corrected after the fact;
- monthly reporting to investors of interest and principal payments received, and any losses, delinquencies, charge-offs, prepayments, or repayments;
- new accounts selection for revolving structures;
- replacement of deficient assets; and
- incorporation of special programs that enable borrowers to skip payments because of holidays or other extensions allowed in a program.

Putting together an asset-backed security is complicated and costly. Investors should become aware of the process to ensure that their interests are being served properly.

Investors should be equally aware of the servicing system and its role in the securitization of assets. For many issuing institutions, the servicing system will be the biggest hurdle to efficient securitization. The costs of time and money may be substantial if existing systems are inadequate. Once systems are made adequate, however, the systems generally require minimal changes.

The complicated nature of the servicing requirements makes careful analysis of the servicing risk imperative. In most cases, this may be the prime concern of credit enhancers taking a risk in enhancing a particular security. Investors should also be aware of these servicing concerns, because except for government-guaranteed assets, there is no servicing standard and a very limited review process. Further, with the advent of cash flow-enhanced transactions, the quality of the servicer is more important to the investor.

Structuring

Proper structuring of asset-backed securities is very important. One of the major innovations in asset-backed securities is the ability to separate the credit of the asset pool from the underlying credit of the institution to protect the investor if a corporation files for bankruptcy. The U.S. Bankruptcy Code applies to most institutions—with the exception of banks and thrifts—and has automatic-stay provisions that usually stop payments of principal and interest to debtholders. Even in situations in which the debt is collateralized, unless ultimate repayment is assured, investors are likely to suffer some delays in payment receipts. In contrast, an asset-backed security can be structured to be a sale of assets (as opposed to debt), thus bypassing bankruptcy entirely.

The key to an asset securitization is the sale of the assets to a special-purpose vehicle, a separate entity that becomes the owner of record of the assets. In setting up the proper ownership, certain precautions must be taken to ensure that the transaction qualifies for obtaining a true sale opinion. The ownership of the assets must be perfected through filing appropriate documents as required by the Uniform Commercial Code, and a special-purpose vehicle must be structured so that it cannot engage in any activity causing it to become bankrupt. If the special-purpose vehicle is a limited-purpose subsidiary of the originating corporation, investors must also be protected from consolidation with the parent in the event of the parent's bankruptcy.

In the case of banks and thrifts, all of these conditions must be met, with the exception of the sale-of-asset provision. These institutions are exempt from the Bankruptcy Code and may pledge assets instead of worrying about a true sale opinion. Note, however, that investors may still have reasons for concern because banks and thrifts can become insolvent and placed in receivership by either the Resolution Trust Corporation (RTC) or the Federal Deposit Insurance Corporation (FDIC). In such a case the RTC or the FDIC may either maintain the security structure or accelerate payments. The passage of the Financial Institutions Reform, Recovery and Enforcement Act of 1989 (FIRREA) has generated further concerns and confusions in the market, so most investors prefer a true sale opinion even for banks and thrifts.

Special-purpose entities may take one of three legal forms: corporations, trusts, or partnerships.

The appropriate form will depend on the federal income tax consequences and the need to restructure cash flows to meet investor demand. Possible vehicles include grantor trusts, which generate pass-through obligations, Real Estate Mortgage Investment Act securities (REMICs), and special-purpose corporations that issue debt, commonly referred to as pay-through bonds.

The simplest way to structure an asset-backed security is to issue a grantor trust. Investors become the beneficial owners of the assets and their subsequent cash flows. This is achieved by the originator depositing assets in the trust in exchange for pass-through certificates. A basic premise of the trust is that the cash flows are passed through to the investor unaltered. Otherwise, the trust must be treated as a taxable entity, thus lowering the cash flow available to investors. Grantor trust vehicles allow for limited restructuring of cash flows. Interest payments can be segregated to support servicing or credit enhancement, or can be stripped and sold independently to investors. Junior and senior ownership structures are acceptable, but any other reallocation of principal payments is not allowed. Typical grantor trusts are Ginnie Mae, Federal National Mortgage Association (Fannie Mae), and Federal Home Loan Mortgage Corporation (Freddie Mac) securities. In essence, a grantor trust pass-through security retains the basic characteristics of the underlying asset and should be analyzed as such.

The REMIC, introduced in 1987, enabled issuers to generate multiple-class and multiple-maturity mortgage securities, which led to the growth of the collateralized mortgage obligation (CMO) market. Multiple-class and multiple-maturity structures, such as CMOs, are attractive because cash flows can be segregated and sold separately to various investors. Previously CMOs had been restricted to corporations issuing debt, such as Freddie Mac. The REMIC structure is only available to mortgages, however, not other assets.

Pay-through structures constitute the vehicle for cash flow structuring of nonmortgage asset-backed securities. This issuance vehicle is debt, generated by a special-purpose corporation or trust. The entity purchases assets and then issues debt structures similar to a CMO. With the absence of an REMIC exemption, the entity will be taxed according to its legal structure. These debt vehicles are called pay-through bonds, but keep in mind that the term refers to transactions that can be structured as true sale transactions to the issuer even though they may be debt to the special-purpose subsidiary. The reason for the pay-through debt structure is to avoid double taxation with a special-purpose vehicle, in which both the income of the assets and the owner's equity would be taxed.

Pay-through bonds may be highly leveraged, but there must be equity for tax purposes. Equity may be in the form of ownership, residual cash flow, a seller's interest, or direct equity investment. Required levels of equity are determined according to tax considerations. Structural trade-offs may be necessary, and issuers may have to make choices between limitation of the ownership of residuals versus additional tax liability. Although these considerations have not severely limited the asset-backed market, they generate costs eliminated from mortgage securitization after the introduction of REMICs.

The final feature of the asset-backed securitization structure is credit enhancement. Once a transaction structure has been determined, the expected cash flows are analyzed to determine the appropriate level of credit enhancement. Because the underlying assets are expected to incur some loss, investors and rating agencies require some form of credit enhancement to cover expected losses. If the assets are relatively small, statistical procedures are used to determine worst-case loss scenarios based on historical data: delinquencies, losses, and charge-offs for payments and repayments. Also taken into account are the underlying criteria of the servicing characteristics: quality, demographic characteristics of the portfolio, borrower profile, and economic analysis of the geographic region. Statistical procedures are not completely adequate to analyze pools of large assets, so the relative impact and weighting of each asset must be analyzed independently. The perceived risk in the portfolio may be eliminated through credit enhancement structures that provide additional sources of funds to cover losses or temporary shortfalls.

A key concern for many issuers is the accounting for credit enhancement mechanism so that it does not jeopardize the true sale status. Generally Accepted Accounting Principles (GAAP) under FASB 77 allow for the sale of assets with limited recourse to the issuer if the obligations under recourse can be reasonably estimated and the issuer is not required to repurchase the assets. Although most corporations' financial statements are prepared according to GAAP, financial institutions must also be concerned with Regulatory Accounting Principles (RAP). According to RAP, banks and thrifts may not achieve true sale of assets if there is any form of recourse, with the exception of a recourse related to mortgage assets.

Credit enhancement may take may take several forms, which can be divided into those that rely on the financial strength of a credit provider and those that depend on a restructuring and segregation of the cash flows.

In general, credit providers must have a rating at least as strong as the rating anticipated on the transaction. Recourse to the seller or a guarantee by the seller up to a certain percentage of the transaction is generally seen as the most cost-effective method of credit enhancement. This form of self-insurance is attractive to many highly rated corporations, but is generally not acceptable to banks because it would not provide for a sale treatment under RAP.

Bank letters of credit and third-party guarantees are provided by highly rated financial institutions. Such guarantees may be as low as 5 percent of the face amount of the issue or as high as 100 percent by insurance companies providing surety bonds. The leading AAA credit enhancers include Union Bank of Switzerland and Credit Suisse, who provide letters of credit, and Financial Guaranty Insurance Company (FGIC) and Financial Security Assurance, Inc. (FSA), who provide surety bonds.

Credit enhancement may also take the form of subordinated interest created from restructuring the cash flow of the assets into a senior/subordinate structure. Defaults and losses would be first attributed to the subordinate piece, thus providing protection for the senior certificates. Typically an issuer will hold the subordinate piece or sell it as a private placement. This qualifies as a sale for a corporation in both cases, and for a bank only if the subordinate piece is sold.

Overcollateralization and reserve accounts are another way of obtaining credit enhancement by designating or creating special assets to absorb any credit losses. Additional assets may be added to support the transaction, or in the case of reserve accounts, generated by the excess of the money earned on the receivables over the amount paid to coupon holders, and to providers of other services. This excess cash flow from either a reserve account or overcollateralization may be augmented by other deposits and used independently or in conjunction with a corporation or third-party guarantee.

Overcollateralization and reserve account structures qualify as a true sale under GAAP, and only under RAP if expenses are taken up front.

Various combinations of techniques may be used, but if a primary credit enhancer exists, some of the other techniques are used to protect the credit enhancer and not the investor.

Rating agencies play a major role in securitized transactions. Rating agencies play a more passive role in the rating process under typical debt structures, but are active participants in the securitization process. A review of the servicer, the collateral, the cash flow structure, and the legal structure will determine whether the situation is bankruptcy remote and whether the issuing entity has perfected the security interest in the receivable. The rating agency then determines the degree of credit enhancement necessary to achieve a targeted rating.

Investors will be concerned with many of the same issues and are advised to scrutinize carefully the rating agency's list of criteria as well as develop their own criteria. Investors might also be concerned with the quality of the credit enhancer and the likelihood of downgrade, the volume of issuance by a particular issue or type of structure, and whether the structural issues are particularly attractive to only one group of investors.

Conclusion

Intelligent people may disagree about who will be the survivors in the securitization phenomenon, but few can afford to avoid the evolution. Investors, managers of financial institutions, and regulators are closely watching this emerging market. The needs, concerns, and relative market clout of each group will add to the complexity of this evolving structure, and will likely generate temporary imbalances and inefficiencies in the marketplace. Any major technological change will disrupt the status quo and generate new winners and losers in the competitive marketplace, but no matter how painful or inequitable it may appear in the short run, technological change cannot be stopped, and it would be fruitless to delay unnecessarily. Astute market participants would be advised to follow this evolution closely, helping to shape the future of this technological revolution.

Valuation Challenges: Mortgage-Backed Securities and Collateralized Mortgage Obligations

Scott F. Richard
Vice President, Fixed Income Research
Goldman, Sachs & Co.

The valuation of mortgage-backed securities and collateralized mortgage obligations (CMOs) involves many challenges. At Goldman Sachs, we value mortgages using a simulation model that is based on a term structure model and a prepayment model. In this presentation, I will discuss these models and how they are used to value mortgage-backed securities. Because CMOs are simply a regrouping of the cash flows from mortgage-backed securities, the valuation of CMO tranches will follow directly from the valuation of mortgage-backed securities.

Simulation Method

Simulation is more than just intuitively appealing; in mortgage-backed securities it is absolutely crucial. Simulation is used as a valuation method for three reasons. First, cash flows are path dependent for mortgage-backed securities; in other words, you have to know if interest rates were high or low in the past to determine today's and future cash flows.

The second reason to use simulation is that CMOs are very complicated instruments. Some have been issued with over 25 tranches in a deal. Think of the tranches as people standing in a line. What the fifth person gets for this month's cash flow depends on how many people are standing in line in front of him. It is not possible to figure out what the cash flow will be to tranche five unless we know what happened to tranches one through four. To figure out what happened to those tranches, we must know what their outstanding balances are, which means we have to know all the prepayments made to date.

The third reason to use simulation is that adjustable-rate mortgages are also path dependent when they have reset rate caps. If an adjustable-rate mortgage's coupon is going to reset this month and it has a collar—that is, it cannot reset more than 200 basis points up or down relative to where it was a year

ago—then this means we must keep track of where it was a year ago, which is also a path dependency. These are some of the additional complications of looking at mortgages as opposed to modeling other types of fixed-income securities.

In principle, the valuation of mortgages is very simple. In practice, it is very complex: because the cash flows are not specified, they must be simulated. The simulation involves generating a set of cash flows based on simulated interest rates, which in turn imply simulated prepayment rates. Take, for example, a newly issued 30-year mortgage-backed security. This security generates 30 years (360 months) of cash flows, but the cash flows depend on future interest rates. The monthly cash flows are simulated based on estimates of the monthly interest rates. The value of the mortgage is the present value of the monthly cash flows. In Goldman Sachs's valuation model, the procedure is repeated 1,024 times, and the results are averaged to get the model's estimate of the security's value. The number of repetitions determines the variance of the estimated value. (We use a variance-reduction technique so that only 1,024 iterations are required to complete the calculation with the precision we require.)

The estimated monthly interest rates are generated from random drawings from arbitrage-free models of the term structure of interest rates. By arbitrage-free, I mean the model replicates the on-the-run Treasury valuation, which is an input to the model, and that for all future dates there is no arbitrage possible within the model. An arbitrage-free model of Treasury yields means that at all future dates within the model the price of any long-term bond equals the expected present value of rolling short-term bonds to the same maturity.[1] For example, you

---

[1] For details, see F. Black, E. Derman, and W. Toy, "A One-Factor Model of Interest Rates and Its Application to Treasury Bond Options." New York: Goldman, Sachs & Co. (1988).

could not have negative forward rates at any time over the next 30 years. The model also generates the estimated refinancing or mortgage rate for each month. The monthly cash flows are simple to conceptualize, but estimating them is difficult.

Credit risk has not been a major factor in the valuation of mortgage-backed securities, which are predominantly issued by Ginnie Mae, Fannie Mae, and Freddie Mac. Ginnie Mae (Government National Mortgage Association) is a U.S. government agency, backed by the full faith and credit of the U.S. government. Fannie Mae (Federal National Mortgage Association) and Freddie Mac (Federal Home Loan Mortgage Corporation) are special private corporations that have implicit government guarantees and explicit $2 billion lines of credit with the Treasury.

Prepayment risk is the most important risk for purchasers of mortgage-backed securities. The trick to evaluating mortgage-backed securities is to get the prepayments right. Our model estimates prepayments based on the interest rate scenario. Thus, the monthly cash flow estimates reflect the scheduled amortization, scheduled interest payments, and prepayments. Mortgages are difficult to evaluate because their value depends on interest rate paths. For example, prepayments depend not only on current interest rates, but also on the interest rate history of the mortgage. Mortgage holders would do different things today if the path of interest rates went higher and then lower, as opposed to lower and then higher.

Term-Structure Model

Two major building blocks are involved in valuing mortgages: the term-structure model and the prepayment model. The term-structure model is used to generate interest rates. Our model assumes that the short-term interest rate follows a geometric random walk.[2] In other words, the current term structure is used as the market's forecast of where future rates will go, with the same probabilities of being an equal percentage above and below those forecasts. Typically, probabilities are presented in the form of a tree, similar to that shown in **Figure 1**. This creates an arbitrage-free pricing of Treasury zero-coupon bonds of all maturities. Thus, if you want to value a 30-year mortgage, a 360-month tree would be generated from which the simulations would be drawn.

The inputs to the model are the current prices of Treasury bonds plus an estimate of interest rate volatility. Volatility is very important because mortgage-

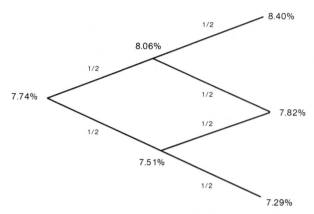

Figure 1. Section of Interest Rate Tree

Note: Annual short-rate volatility = 12 percent

Source: Goldman, Sachs & Co.

backed securities have an option embedded in them, and the value of the option is related to volatility. In Figure 1, volatility is assumed to be 12 percent per year. These numbers are the one-month interest rates that would replicate the term structure on September 20, 1990, assuming 12 percent volatility. On September 20, the one-month rate was 7.74 percent. What the one-month rate will be one month later is not known, but if it is equally likely to be 8.06 percent or 7.51 percent, then this is equivalent to an annual volatility of 12 percent.

In essence, the path of interest rates is simulated by a series of coin flips. Starting at the beginning node with the current rate of 7.74 percent, we can either go up to 8.06 percent if the coin is "heads" or down to 7.51 percent if the coin is "tails." There are no views built into the model about where interest rates are going, other than the market's views which are implicit in today's term structure. It is only the market's view plus the volatility assumption that determines the future paths of interest rates.

Prepayment Model

The other major building block is a prepayment model. Homeowners do all sorts of unexpected things every month—they prepay mortgages that have very low interest rates and take out mortgages with higher interest rates. For example, they will prepay a 7 percent loan, because they are moving, and replace it with a loan at 10 or 11 percent. Why would anybody exercise the option to prepay when it is deep out of the money? On the other hand, many people

[2]The model was developed by Fischer Black, Emmanuel Derman, and William Toy.

have loans bearing interest rates of 14 percent or more but have not exercised their deep-in-the-money options! Currently there are $1 billion of outstanding Ginnie Mae 14s and above. Why do homeowners keep them when they could replace them with 9 or 10 percent loans? To explain prepayments, which are critical to estimating the cash flows from a mortgage, you have to think about what the homeowner is doing. You have to think about what part of their behavior you can rationally explain, and what part of their behavior cannot be predicted as a rational response to the economic environment.

We use an empirical approach to model homeowner prepayment decisions, taking into account factors such as interest rates and the age of the mortgage loan. The model is multiplicative in four effects: (1) the refinancing incentive, (2) the age of the mortgage or seasoning, (3) the month of the year or seasonality, and (4) what is called "premium burn out." Premium mortgages tend to go through a spiking period when they see a rally: prepayment rates go very high, then burn out and slow down even though mortgage rates have not risen.

The refinancing rate affects prepayment rates. **Figure 2** illustrates the effect on prepayments as the incentive to refinance increases. The incentive to refinance is measured as the difference between the homeowner's weighted average coupon (WAC) within the mortgage-backed security pool minus the current refinancing (Refi) rate. This measures consumers' incentives to prepay or to not prepay. Discount loans are to the left, and premium loans are to the right, of where WAC minus Refi is zero. The conventional mortgages are those backing the pools issued by Fannie Mae and Freddie Mac; the FHA/VA mortgages are those backing the pools issued by Ginnie Mae. The Fannie Mae and Freddie Mac curve—the conventional curve—is estimated from data starting from the middle of 1982; the FHA/VA curve is based on data starting in 1980. Figure 2 shows that current coupon (WAC – Refi = 0) Ginnie Maes prepay at a rate of about 6 percent per year, and current coupon conventionals prepay at about 9 percent.

People prepay mortgages that are below market for a variety of reasons—the five "D's": departure, death, divorce, destruction, and default. Except for departure and default, which might be related to the market price of housing, these explanations have little to do with market interest rates; they are demographic or have something to do with the idiosyncratic behavior of a household.

The premium mortgages have much higher prepayment rates. Many people will choose to prepay at 300 or 400 basis points into the money so that conventional mortgages will prepay at a rate of about 50 percent of the outstanding pool per year, and the FHA/VA Ginnie Mae mortgages will prepay at about 40 percent. The question, however, is, "Why doesn't everybody prepay so that when the WAC minus Refi is above 400 basis points, the pools will have disappeared altogether?"

Several reasons explain why people do not prepay these loans. One reason is that the borrower has lost his job and no longer qualifies for a new loan. Another reason could be that the value of the house has declined to a level that is lower than the mortgage value. In this case, if the borrower prepays the premium mortgage, he must also raise enough cash to cover the difference between the outstanding value of the home and the outstanding balance on the loan, therefore giving up the valuable right to put the house to the bank (i.e., default). Finally, there just seems to be a large group of people who are not rational. These folks are the ones who hold these high-premium loans and choose not to prepay them, even in the face of repeated efforts to get them to do so.[3]

A year ago April, the undersecretary of Housing and Urban Development (HUD) wrote a letter to all the individuals holding Ginnie Mae 14s and above, stating more or less that "You have a premium mortgage, you should prepay it. Look up 'Mortgages' in the yellow pages." The letter did give one useful piece of information—it said you automatically requalify.

Figure 2. Seasonally Adjusted and Fully Seasoned Prepayment Rates

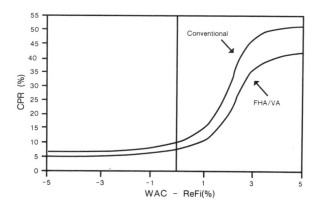

Source: Goldman, Sachs & Co.

---

[3]There may be two groups that make sense. If you have a low loan balance and your payment is $50 and refinancing will only cut it to $40, taking the time to file the application may not be worth saving $10 a month. Also, we know that some of the Ginnie Mae high-coupon pools contain subsidized mortgages so that the homeowners in these pools have diminished incentives to prepay.

In effect, it said, we don't care if you are on your deathbed, out of work, or where your house is located, you automatically requalify for a lower-coupon current mortgage. Why would HUD do that? HUD insures the FHA/VA programs, and is responsible for making up the losses. Therefore, HUD benefited because almost all of its defaults were in these high-coupon loans, so they were better off if these homeowners could be induced to refinance. The mortgage originators were delighted to originate new loans and take the points. The homeowner was better off because his payments would be cut substantially. Of course, the people who were left holding the bag were the mortgage-backed security holders, because they had a premium loan priced at 104 or 106 that was going to be prepaid at par. As it turned out, however, there was no discernible change in the prepayment pattern as a result of HUD's letter. This makes it clear that the people who have not taken the opportunity to refinance their 14 percent mortgages are not likely to do it in any great number, which is why we call it the "burn out" effect.

Another factor that affects prepayments is seasoning, which is the tendency of mortgage prepayment rates to increase as time passes, not because rates have changed. The reasoning behind seasoning is that homeowners take a while to either reaccumulate the money for points for refinancing or to get the kind of incentives necessary to get them to move again. **Figure 3** depicts a plausible seasoning pattern (usually referred to as a PSA model, which is simply a nomenclature by which everyone can discuss the seasoning of mortgages in a common vocabulary). The standard, or 100 percent PSA model, is a steadily increasing prepayment rate from zero percent at inception to 6 percent at 30 months, after which the rate remains constant at 6 percent. When analysts speak of 200 percent PSA, they mean double that prepayment rate pattern, and 50 PSA means half of the rate.

Discounts, current, and premium mortgages season differently. Current coupons take around 40 months to season. **Figure 4** shows that a current Ginnie Mae mortgage-backed security with a 9 percent coupon rate would have a 3 percent projected prepayment rate if it was only half seasoned—i.e., 20 months old. Discount mortgages season over long periods of time because often a long period of time is required for the right kind of economic event to occur which will prompt people to move. Premiums season more rapidly; the inducement to move or prepay is greater when you have a gain from prepaying your mortgage on top of everything else.

In addition to the seasoning effect, there is a monthly effect. Investors must keep in mind that seasonal changes exist in prepayments and that seasonal variation should not be confused with a secular effect. The same monthly variation occurs in warm states like California or Texas as occurs in Massachusetts or Maine because of the school year. Therefore, we estimate monthly multipliers to slightly adjust the rate up or down each month. These multipliers are relatively small and do not affect value very much in any mortgage-backed security. **Figure 5** shows the monthly multipliers for Fannie Maes. March has the lowest adjustment, about 0.84; September has the highest, 1.16.

One of the effects that we try to pick up is the tendency for premium mortgages to hit a peak and then

Figure 3. PSA Prepayment Model

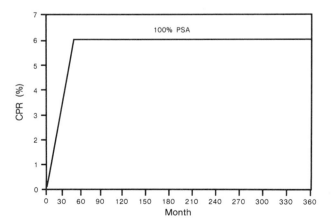

Source: Goldman, Sachs & Co.

Figure 4. Ginnie Mae Seasoning

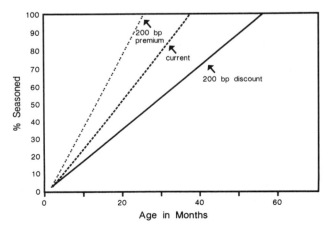

Source: Goldman, Sachs & Co.

Figure 5. Federal National Mortgage Association Monthly Prepayment Multipliers

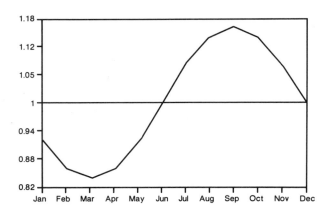

Source: Goldman, Sachs & Co.

Figure 6. Response to 300 Basis Point Decline in Rates: Current 10s on January 19, 1990

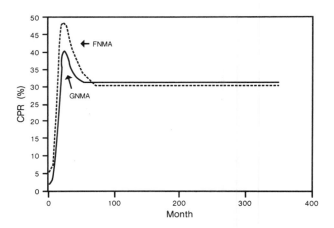

Source: Goldman, Sachs & Co.

burn out. In January 1990, the current coupon Ginnie Mae and Fannie Mae was 10 percent. **Figure 6** shows our model's prediction for prepayment rates on these securities if interest rates had rallied 300 basis points over the next year. The Fannie Maes would peak at about a 50 percent prepayment rate and then burn out at about 30 percent. Ginnie Maes would peak at 40 percent and then burn out at about 30 percent. This pattern reflects the fact that interest-sensitive people exit the pool to refinance, or to move and refinance, in the early months, leaving the people who like their high-coupon mortgages.

The prepayment model generates prepayment rate projections for various interest rate scenarios. **Figure 7** illustrates the prepayment rates for Fannie Mae 9s on September 28, 1990. The WAC in the pool is 10.1 percent, and the maturity is 356 months, so these are newly issued mortgages. The current coupon yield was 9.82 percent, so homeowners would pay around 75 basis points above that to refinance. If there is no change in interest rates, the mortgage-backed security just seasons and reaches its plateau prepayment rate of around 9 percent. If a 150-basis-point rally occurs in the first year, the prepayment rate will rise quickly to around 17 percent and then level off. In a 300-basis-point rally, the prepayment rate rises quickly, and then falls back somewhat—the spike-and-burn pattern. In the sell-off scenarios where mortgage rates rise 150 or 300 basis points, prepayment rates slow. This is very undesirable to the mortgage-backed security investor because the security is now at a discount and prepayments are received at par. The speeding of prepayment rates in a rally and the slowing of prepayment rates in a sell-off

are the source of negative convexity in mortgage-backed securities.

Option-Adjusted Spread

The prepayment model's output is fed into the term-structure model, which generates the option-adjusted spread (OAS), the yield over the Treasury curve which reconciles the simulation value with the market price. The OAS is a guide to determine which securities are cheap and which are rich. For example, if the market price of a mortgage is 97, but the model

Figure 7. Scenario Prepayment Rates (Fannie Mae 9.5s on September 28, 1990)

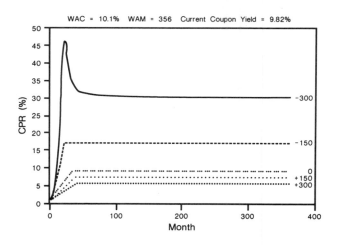

Source: Goldman, Sachs & Co.

estimates it to be worth 98, we can tell people that it is $1 cheap. Conversely, if the market price is 99, we would say that it is $1 rich. In the case where the mortgage is $1 cheap, the OAS will be positive, and if value is less than price, then the bond will be rich and the OAS will be negative.

Clients in the investment industry prefer that value be expressed in terms of yield rather than in terms of dollar price. The OAS is our way of restating dollars rich or cheap into yield loss or gain.

The OAS is calculated using the following formula:

$$P = \frac{1}{1024} \sum_{i=1}^{1024} \left[\frac{C_1(i)}{1 + r_1(i) + Z} + \cdots + \frac{C_{360}(i)}{(1 + r_1 + Z) \ldots (1 + r_{360}(i) + Z)} \right],$$

where Z is the option-adjusted spread, P equals the market price, C equals the cash flow, and r is the monthly Treasury discount rate. There is a cash flow for each month, and a Treasury discount rate that corresponds with the month. The OAS, Z, is the additional yield needed to discount the cash flows to equate exactly model value to the market price, P. If value is too high, Z will be positive; if the value is too low, Z will be negative.

Using the OAS Model

The OAS model can be used to evaluate mortgage-backed securities. **Figure 8** shows the OASs on September 27, 1990, at 12 percent volatility, for a 30-year Fannie Mae pool. The current coupon, which was 9.5 percent, was around 52 basis points cheaper than an equivalent Treasury, or 52 basis points over the yield curve. What could be some of the reasons? As coupon increases, OAS becomes tighter to the curve, and as coupon decreases, OAS becomes wider (with the exception that the 8s are pretty rich that day). Would you want to trade on these numbers? Are they the real indication of value?

An OAS sector profile helps answer these questions. **Figure 9** presents an OAS sector profile for Fannie Mae 30-year mortgage-backed securities. The asterisk shows where the current spread is, the dot shows the average spread, and the vertical line depicts the range over the last 90 days. Currently the OASs are on the tight side, in the lower half of the last 90-day range. From a technical point of view, they do not look like they are cheap relative to where they have been trading. As an investor, you should look at where mortgages have been over some historical period relative to where they are now.

The option-adjusted spreads will change if the prepayment pattern changes. **Figure 10** shows what happens to 30-year Fannie Mae OASs under different prepayment assumptions, as of September 27, 1990. The figure shows that at 90 percent of the current prepayment rate, the OASs for all coupons become more nearly equal to each other, at around 50 basis points. This may indicate that the market is anticipating a 10 percent slowing of prepayment rates relative to our model. If your view is very bearish on the economy, you may want to run the prepayment model at 80 percent. Instead of concluding that the discounts are the cheap sector, you would conclude that the premiums are the cheap sector because slow premiums are good and slow discounts are bad. Conversely, you might

Figure 8. Thirty-Year Fannie Mae OASs on September 27, 1990

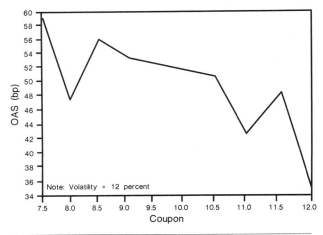

Figure 9. Option-Adjusted Spread Sector Profile: Fannie Mae 30-Year Conventional Single-Family (June 28, 1990 to September 28, 1990)

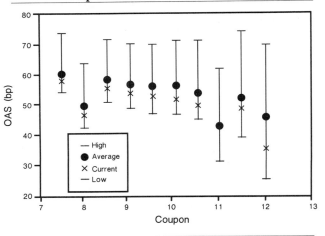

Figure 10. Thirty-Year Fannie Mae OASs under Different Prepayment Assumptions on September 27, 1990

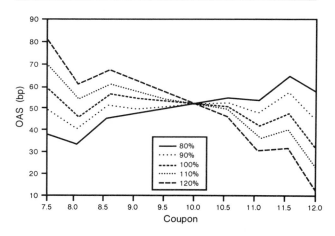

Source: Goldman, Sachs & Co.

have the view that the market is overestimating the size and duration of the recession, and think that prepayment rates will pick up, relative to the model; the effects of these scenarios on OASs are shown by the lines marked 110 percent and 120 percent.

Analyzing what happens to the OAS if the volatility changes is also important. **Figure 11** shows what happens to 30-year Fannie Mae OASs at different volatilities, as of September 27, 1990. The higher the volatility, the worse the mortgage-backed security looks, because holding a mortgage-backed security means you are short an option—the homeowners retain the option to prepay. Hence, as volatility increases, OAS decreases at each coupon. If, for example, you believe volatility has risen from a 12 percent level to 14, you would say the mortgage looked richer than at 12. Conversely, if volatility has decreased, the mortgages look better than at the 12 percent level. Thus, you must ask yourself three questions: (1) What has happened to prepayments relative to this model? (2) What has happened to volatility relative to this model? and (3) Where are OASs in a historical context?

In addition to the option-adjusted spread, the option-adjusted duration and convexity can also be calculated for each mortgage-backed security. In fact, you cannot evaluate a mortgage's sensitivity to shifts in rates without doing the option valuation simultaneously. The static or Macaulay duration and convexity have no bearing on the pricing of mortgage-backed securities because mortgage cash flows vary systematically with interest rates.

Table 1 presents the OAS, option-adjusted duration, and convexity for a range of coupons on 30-year

Fannie Mae mortgage-backed securities. The table shows that the duration goes from 5.33 years for the 7.5 percent coupon to less than two years for the 12 percent coupons. These duration numbers have been tested against empirical moves in the market, and they match extremely well. The durations suggest excellent hedges for traders or give an excellent measure of portfolio interest rate risks for long-term investors. We can empirically measure duration, but convexity must be estimated from the model, because even a tick off the mark on the price can completely change the empirical estimate. Premium mortgages are negatively convex because the owner is short an in-the-money option, whereas discount mortgages are positively convex, although much less positively convex than a Treasury of similar coupon and duration. That is because the option to prepay is very deep out-of-the-money, so the bond actually becomes positively convex instead of negatively convex.

Collateralized Mortgage Obligations

CMOs are a way of restructuring the cash flows from a mortgage-backed security to redistribute the prepayment risk. All of the holders of a mortgage-backed security receive prepayments on a share-and-share-alike basis. In a CMO, some tranches, such as PAC bonds, have little exposure to changes in prepayment rates, whereas other tranches, such as PAC support bonds, bear all or most of the prepayment risk.

To see how the underlying mortgage-backed security collateral is restructured, we look at a deal sheet. **Table 2** is the deal sheet for Freddie Mac 120. Despite its appearance, this is not a particularly complex deal structure. The top half describes each

Table 1. Fannie Mae 30-Year Single Family Mortgage-Backed Securities (September 27, 1990)

Coupon	Option-Adjusted Spread	Option-Adjusted Duration	Option-Adjusted Convexity
7.5	59	5.33	0.11
8.0	47	5.53	0.10
8.5	56	5.29	0.03
9.0	54	5.09	−0.04
9.5	53	4.80	−0.13
10.0	52	4.25	−0.29
10.5	51	3.50	−0.48
11.0	43	2.62	−0.56
11.5	49	2.31	−0.59
12.0	35	1.83	−0.64

Source: Goldman, Sachs & Co.

Table 2. Federal Home Loan Mortgage Corporation: Multiclass Mortgage Participation Certificates (Guaranteed), Series 120

Total issue:	$300,000,000
Issue date:	12/08/89
Structure type:	REMIC CMO
Original rating:	S&P NR, Moody's NR, Fitch NR, D&P NR
Issuer class:	Agency
Dated Date:	1/15/90
Original settlement date:	1/30/90
Payment frequency:	Monthly; 15th day of month

Tranche	Original Balance	Coupon	Stated Maturity	Days Delay	Original Issue Pricing (180.0% PSA Assumed)				
					Price	Yield	Average Life	Expected Maturity	Spread
120-A (PAC Bond)	$37,968,750	16.000%	11/15/13	30	NA	NA	4.0 yr.	12/15/95	NA
120-B (PAC Bond)	$20,500,000	0.000%	2/15/11	30	NA	NA	3.4 yr.	10/15/94	NA
120-C (PAC Bond)	$ 9,031,250	0.000%	11/15/13	30	NA	NA	5.3 yr.	12/15/95	NA
120-D (PAC Bond)	$12,000,000	9.000%	2/15/15	30	NA	NA	6.3 yr.	9/15/96	NA
120-E (PAC Bond)	$40,500,000	9.000%	5/15/18	30	NA	NA	7.9 yr.	7/15/99	NA
120-F (PAC Bond)	$10,000,000	9.000%	1/15/19	30	NA	NA	10.0 yr.	8/15/00	NA
120-G (PAC Bond)	$ 6,500,000	9.000%	6/16/19	30	NA	NA	10.9 yr.	6/15/01	NA
120-H (PAC Bond)	$33,000,000	9.000%	2/15/21	30	NA	NA	15.5 yr.	4/15/18	NA
120-I (PAC Bond)	$ 100,000	857.000%	2/15/21	30	NA	NA	7.9 yr.	4/15/18	NA
120-J (TAC Bond)	$99,600,000	9.500%	2/15/21	30	NA	NA	3.2 yr.	10/15/99	NA
120-K	$15,700,000	9.500%	7/15/15	30	NA	NA	8.3 yr.	7/15/01	NA
120-R	$ 90,000	9.500%	2/15/21	30	NA	NA	8.1 yr.	4/15/19	NA
120-S	$ 10,000	9.500%	2/15/21	30	NA	NA	8.1 yr.	4/15/19	NA
120-Z	$15,000,000	9.500%	2/15/21	30	NA	NA	18.8 yr.	4/15/19	NA

Structural Features:

Prepayment guarantee: None

Assumed reinvestment rate: 0%

Cash flow allocation: Excess cash flow is not anticipated; however, in the event that there are proceeds remaining after the payments of the bonds, the Class 120-R Bonds will receive them. Commencing on the first principal payment date of the Class 120-A Bonds, principal equal to an amount specified in the Prospectus will be applied to the Class 120-A, 120-B, 120-C, 120-D, 120-E, 120-F, 120-G, 120-H, 120-I, and 120-J Bonds. After all other Classes have been retired, any remaining principal will be used to retire the Class 120-J, 120-A, 120-B, 120-C, 120-D, 120-E, 120-F, 120-G, 120-H, and 120-I Bonds.

Principal allocation structure:

120-R					
120-J		120-K		120-Z	
120-I					
120-A		120-D	120-E	120-F	120-G	120-H
120-B	120-C					

Redemption provisions: Nuisance provision for all Classes: Issuer may redeem the Bonds, in whole but not in part, on any Payment Date when the outstanding principal balance declines to less then 1 percent of the original amount.

Other: The PAC range is 90 percent to 300 percent PSA for the A-I bonds, and 200 percent PSA for the Class J Bonds.

Source: Goldman, Sachs & Co.

tranche in the CMO. Included are an accrual bond, which is the Z tranche, an interest-only bond (IO), which is the *I* bond, and various PAC and PAC support bonds, including two PAC principal-only (PO) bonds.

You can recognize the IO as tranche *I* by its very high coupon (857 percent) and the PAC POs, tranches *B* and *C*, by their zero coupons. The block diagram in

Figure 11. Thirty-Year Fannie Mae OASs at Different Volatility Levels on September 27, 1990

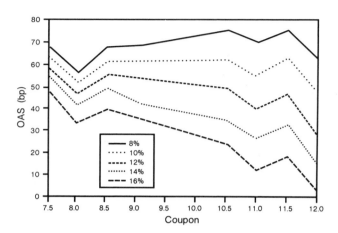

Source: Goldman, Sachs & Co.

the bottom half of Table 2 shows the principal allocation structure for this CMO. The tranches to the left are scheduled to receive principal cash flows before those to the right. The tranches on the top receive unscheduled principal cash flows before those on the bottom.

Because a CMO is just a reallocation of cash flows from the underlying mortgage-backed securities, we can value CMOs using the same simulation model we used for mortgage-backed securities. One additional step is required: We must allocate the simulated monthly cash flows to the tranches. **Figure 12** shows the results of valuing Freddie Mac 120 using the Goldman Sachs valuation model. The figure shows for each tranche the price, yield, average life, option cost in basis points, OAS in basis points, and option-adjusted duration in years.

Just as the cash flows from the collateral are reallocated to the tranches, the collateral OAS is also reallocated to the tranches—but not equally. The collateral for this deal was Freddie Mac mortgage-backed securities with a weighted-average maturity (WAM) of 346 months and a WAC of 10.15 percent. The collateral had an OAS of 57 basis points, but the OASs for the tranches reported in Figure 12 reveal that the value did not get equally distributed. In fact, the *J*, *K*, and *Z* support tranches, which bear most of the prepayment

Figure 12. Analytically Derived CMO Statistics

R		
100-22+	95-19+	83-23+
9.11	10.26	10.78
3.40	10.80	19.10
71.00	61.00	90.00
−15.00	60.00	48.00
3.20	5.60	13.50
J	K	Z

I					
118-03+					
9.16					
3.30					
0.00					
82.00	98-04	97-12+	96-11	95-27+	93-15+
2.40	9.44	9.54	9.66	9.71	9.95
A	5.60	7.30	9.30	10.30	14.80
	1.00	4.00	6.00	6.00	6.00
79-16 / 65-28+	78.00	2.00	71.00	72.00	81.00
8.86 / 9.31	4.10	4.80	5.50	5.80	7.00
2.70 / 4.60					
−3.00 / −7.00					
58.00 / 77.00					
2.70 / 5.00					
B · C	D	E	F	G	H

Note:

Within each block, the numbers are, respectively: Price, Yield, Average Life, Option Cost, Option-Adjusted Spread, and Option-Adjusted Duration. Prices are quoted per $100 of face value in units of dollars and 32nds of a dollar; a plus sign means ¹⁄₆₄ of a dollar.

Source: Goldman, Sachs & Co.

risk, have OASs of –15, 60, and 48, respectively. Tranche *J*, therefore, is rich relative to both the collateral and the yield curve, while tranche *K* is cheap by the same comparison. Similarly, the collateral option cost, which is the difference between the static yield and the OAS, is distributed unevenly across the tranches. For the collateral, the option cost was 36 basis points, but tranches *J* and *K* have larger option costs of 71 and 60 basis points, respectively, whereas the PAC POs (tranches *B* and *C*), of course, have negative option costs.

Although we can apply the same technology to evaluate CMO tranches as we use to evaluate mortgage-backed securities, doing these calculations is very expensive computationally. Until cheaper computation of OASs becomes widely available, investors may have to rely on sophisticated approximations. For example, a tranche's option cost is more stable than its OAS in the face of market movements. Hence, to a good approximation, the OAS on a CMO tranche may be found by recalculating its static yield (which is relatively cheap and easy to calculate) and subtracting its option cost.

Conclusion

The valuation of mortgage-backed securities is simple in concept, but difficult in practice. The simple concept is that value is determined by discounting cash flows over many interest rate scenarios and then averaging the result. The difficulties are in calculating the scenario cash flows, which are estimated using sophisticated prepayment models, and in forecasting likely paths of future interest rates. Once the model value is determined we can compare it to market price to discover which securities are rich and which are cheap. Usually the rich/cheap valuation results are restated in terms of yields by assigning each security an option-adjusted spread. Additional benefits of the valuation model are proper measurement of security interest rate sensitivity by option-adjusted duration and option-adjusted convexity.

The valuation of CMOs is just like the valuation of mortgage-backed securities, only more so. A CMO is the restructuring of the cash flows from mortgage-backed securities into CMO tranches to reallocate prepayment risk. All of the valuation and sensitivity measures developed for mortgage-backed securities—OAS, option-adjusted duration, and option-adjusted convexity—can be calculated for CMO tranches using the same valuation model. These calculations, however, are currently very expensive, and, therefore, sophisticated approximations may have to be used in their stead.

Question and Answer Session

Question: Please elaborate on how you calculated duration.

Richard: The duration is based on rerunning the model at the same option-adjusted spread but with a term structure shifted up 100 basis points. So it is the percentage change in price per 100 basis points change in yield.

Question: In your analysis, does the refinance rate include the points that are charged up front?

Richard: The points are capitalized into the rate.

Question: The CPR (conditional prepayment rate) curve seems to indicate that individuals will respond equally to a change in interest rate from 2 percent to 3 percent as compared to an interest rate change of 10 percent to 11 percent. Is that empirically found to be true?

Richard: Our original model included the ratio of the coupon to the Refi. In theory, coupon relative to Refi would be a better approximation across a wider range of rates. Empirically, it is very difficult to distinguish. We have tried the two. The coefficients of determination (i.e., R^2) are almost identical. If we ever get a regime where we have 2 percent rates and 20 percent rates, then we will be able to settle this issue. Our data cover a period of time where mortgage rates ranged from a low of around 8 percent to a high of around 15 or 16 percent. Believe it or not, this is not extreme enough to see whether there is a level effect or whether you can just look at the difference.

Question: Is there any difference between the prepayment rates according to loan size? For example, would a $100,000 mortgage loan prepay faster or slower than a $50,000 loan?

Richard: So far we have found that the size of the loan does not affect the average prepayment rate level, but large pools have less monthly variance in their prepayment rates because there are more homeowners in the pool to make behavior more predictable.

Question: Please describe how you calculate a 12 percent volatility.

Richard: In theory, you want to build a process for volatility, because volatility itself is volatile. We get the volatility from the market by looking at the implied yield volatility from the bond future, which is the short volatility. For the longer volatility, we look at the implied volatility in the cap and the swaption markets. These numbers are used as inputs to our model to figure out as best we can where the long-term volatility for the short rate will be.

Strategies for Using Derivative Mortgage-Backed Securities in Pension Portfolios

Kenneth B. Dunn
Partner
Miller, Anderson & Sherrerd

The development of the mortgage-backed securities market about 20 years ago was a major financial innovation that has benefits for many types of investors. It has grown dramatically and now comprises a spectrum of securities ranging from the basic mortgage-backed securities issued by the Government National Mortgage Association (Ginnie Mae), the Federal National Mortgage Association (Fannie Mae), and the Federal Home Loan Mortgage Association (Freddie Mac) to the more complicated derivative mortgage-backed securities. Some examples of derivative mortgage-backed securities are interest-only strips (IOs), principal-only strips (POs), planned amortization class bonds (PACs), targeted amortization class bonds (TACs), accrual bonds (Z-bonds), and a variety of other collateralized mortgage obligations (CMOs). Some of these securities are particularly attractive to investors because they can be used to improve the payoff pattern and risk/return characteristics of a portfolio.

This presentation provides a general framework for evaluating derivative mortgage-backed securities. For convenience, I will use CMO to refer to derivative mortgage-backed securities in general, including IOs and POs. First I will discuss some properties of derivative mortgage-backed securities, whether the mortgage index is an efficient portfolio, and the role of models in designing and structuring portfolios. Once I have laid this foundation, I will discuss how CMOs can be used in pension portfolios and present some simple tools for evaluating CMOs. I assume a basic familiarity with mortgage valuation (option-adjusted spread) models.

Properties of CMOs

Overall, CMOs have been an important financial innovation, but they have both good and bad aspects. The good features include their role in integrating the mortgage market with the corporate and Treasury bond markets, and in reallocating risk. CMOs, particularly those with PAC bonds, make mortgages look more like corporate and Treasury bonds, allowing them to compete more directly for capital in the financial markets. By linking the mortgage market to the corporate and Treasury markets, CMOs limit the extent that mortgages can become cheap relative to corporate and Treasury bonds. Homeowners benefit directly from this improved integration of the capital market because they are able to obtain mortgages at a lower cost.

The success of CMOs is the result of the ability of investment bankers to restructure and slice mortgages into pieces that appeal to different types of investors. In particular, prepayment risk is reallocated across the various tranches within the CMO structure. Of course, the overall risk does not go away; rather, it is reallocated and concentrated in some CMO tranches, such as support bonds, to create other less-risky tranches. Theoretically, these structures allocate the risk to those who are most willing to bear it, and, therefore, require a lower risk premium. Such investors pay a higher price for the CMO bonds. This creates an arbitrage between CMOs and the underlying collateral (mortgage-backed securities), which then causes mortgage-backed securities to appreciate in value.

In some cases, however, it appears that risk is allocated to those who are unaware of the risks they are accepting. Such investors also pay a high price for the CMO bonds. Sometimes this provides an opportunity for others to purchase cheap bonds from the same deal, but Wall Street firms capture most of the excess profit from selling rich bonds. In contrast to several years ago when CMOs were relatively new, the arbitrage profit that Wall Street firms earn from creating them has declined substantially, making it more difficult for investors to purchase cheap CMOs. The money management business is very competitive. The stronger investors survive and the weaker ones do not, so over time it becomes more difficult to find cheap bonds as the better investors increase their understanding of the securities and the losers are eliminated. In the 1980s, S&Ls provided significant profit opportunities, but those days are over.

A negative aspect of CMOs is the tendency for some of these securities and structures to be so complicated that it is difficult to identify where the options and risks have been hidden. In order to create the most highly valued types of tranches, there is often a remainder that contains complex contingent payoffs or options that are difficult to evaluate. Wall Street is similar to a butcher shop that tries to find creative ways to increase the profits from selling its scraps. Overall, this is a constructive process, but sometimes investors permit the experimentation to go too far. For example, some on Wall Street suggest that CMOs with 13 or more tranches enable them to meet the particular needs of the buyers interested in these securities. But I wonder if 13 tranches are really needed to accomplish this objective. Perhaps with a large number of tranches there is a much better chance of hiding the bad parts so that somebody will unwittingly end up paying too much for some of the bonds. Wall Street, however, would not create these structures if they could not be sold profitably; therefore, it is investors, not Wall Street, that ultimately determine the type of CMOs that are issued.

Another negative aspect of CMOs is their relative lack of liquidity. A mortgage-backed security combines a number of illiquid homeowner mortgages into a standardized package that is very liquid. The CMO partially reverses this process by slicing liquid mortgage-backed securities into a variety of nonstandard and, therefore, less liquid pieces. The more complex the CMO structure and the more small tranches it contains, the greater the loss of liquidity. Any bond from a complex structure suffers a loss of liquidity because in order to evaluate that bond, it is necessary to understand how it interacts with other bonds in the CMO structure. In general, I recommend avoiding complex structures with a lot of small tranches.

In evaluating an individual tranche of a CMO, it is important to determine whether the payoff pattern embodied in that tranche has a useful role in a portfolio. If it does, then it is easier to justify adding it to the portfolio. On the other hand, the only way to justify buying some esoteric securities, such as jump-Zs, is if they are so cheap that there is substantial compensation for bearing some extra risk or incurring additional hedging costs and for being willing to hold them for a long time. Patience is especially important because one should not count on being able to sell these securities at attractive levels in the near future.

Instead, the extra return is likely to be earned from these securities' cash flows over time.

Properties of CMO Prices

CMO pricing adheres to three basic rules: (1) at issuance the value of the pieces is greater than the value of the collateral—the underlying mortgage-backed securities; (2) after issuance, the value of the pieces is less than the value of the collateral; and (3) the bid for a derivative mortgage-backed security will not exceed the cost of making a new one. Consequently, CMOs lose value immediately following issuance.

Issuers earn a profit by slicing mortgage-backed securities into tranches and making CMOs. This profit, which investors must pay for, compensates the issuers for constructing the CMOs. Therefore, the cost of the securities at issuance must exceed the cost of the underlying collateral. But just as a new car depreciates as soon as it is driven out of the showroom, the value of the total CMO falls below the value of the underlying collateral after issuance. As long as collateral is available for making a new CMO, the bid for a tranche of an existing CMO will not exceed the cost of making a new one. Also, because the pieces of a CMO are less liquid than the underlying mortgage-backed securities, the pieces should be less valuable. Hence, after the deal is sold, the sum of the bids for all of the pieces will be less than the value of the underlying collateral. However, the amount by which the sum of the value of the pieces can be less than the value of the underlying collateral is limited by the ability to recombine the deals. This force is stronger for relatively simple deals that are easier to recombine.

This loss of value after issuance does not imply that CMOs destroy value. CMOs have increased the value of the underlying collateral. Thus, the value of the pieces of a CMO is less than the value of the collateral, given that CMOs have increased the value of the collateral; but, the value of the pieces of a CMO may exceed what the value of the collateral would have been if CMOs did not exist.

Implications for Trading Strategies

These properties of CMO prices raise some interesting trading strategy issues. For example, should CMOs be purchased at issuance, or is it best to wait and buy after issuance? On the surface, the better strategy appears to be to wait and buy after issuance. By waiting, however, one encounters an adverse-selection or lemons problem similar to that faced when purchasing a used car. Why has this particular piece not sold yet? If it was sold, why is someone trying to unload it shortly after issuance? What have they learned after purchasing it that makes them want to sell it so quickly? This adverse-selection problem must be traded off against the small premium paid at the time of issuance. There is, however, another problem with purchasing at issuance if the collateral for the deal has not been identified: The dealer has a strong incentive to use the cheapest collateral, and this may hurt some pieces of the CMO more than others.

In practice, the deck is stacked against one's ability to purchase CMOs that are cheaper than the underlying collateral. Also, the transaction costs (bid-ask spreads) are larger for CMOs than for the underlying mortgage-backed securities. Therefore, CMOs are generally an expensive way of replicating the mortgage index. But, as I argue below, most investors should not want to replicate the mortgage index. Overall, CMOs are useful for improving the payoff pattern of a mortgage portfolio, and they may be a cheap way of replicating the cash flows of corporate or Treasury bonds.

Is the Mortgage Index an Efficient Portfolio?

The Shearson Lehman and Salomon Brothers mortgage indexes are portfolios designed to represent the market for agency mortgage-backed securities, so their composition is determined by the outstanding supply of mortgage-backed securities. Although an index is very useful for gauging the return from a passive investment in the mortgage market, in general, indexes are not optimal or efficient portfolios. There is no particular reason for trying to construct portfolios to replicate an index unless the index is an efficient portfolio.

Variance is not a complete measure of risk for the mortgage portion of a portfolio, so assessing the efficiency of the mortgage index in terms of the historical mean and variance of returns omits some important considerations. The covariability of the mortgage portion of the portfolio with the other components of the portfolio is an important factor. Many investors rely on their fixed-income portfolios to hedge bad states of the world relative to their stock portfolios, but the mortgage index has too much call risk to play this role. For example, in a deflationary environment in which interest rates and stock prices fall dramatically, the mortgage index would significantly underperform an equal-duration Treasury bond because the mortgages would be refinanced and the proceeds from these prepayments would have to be reinvested at lower interest rates.

Callability and the resulting negative convexity undermines the role of bonds in an overall portfolio that includes stocks and bonds. The call option embedded in a bond can be divided into two parts. The bad part is that the interest payments are truncated by the call, and the good part is that the principal balance is repaid at the time of the call instead of at maturity. Thus, IOs contain the bad part of the call option and POs contain the good part. Relative to a portfolio with the desired payoff pattern, the mortgage index effectively contains too many IOs and too few POs. To create a more convex payoff for a mortgage portfolio, some POs or other convex derivative mortgage-backed securities can be added to the portfolio to offset some of the negative convexity of the mortgages. Often, the resulting portfolio has a better rate of return profile than that available from a Treasury portfolio.

Unfortunately, some clients and consultants evaluate fixed-income portfolio managers in terms of their excess return per unit of standard deviation relative to some benchmark index, as one might evaluate an equity manager. This approach encourages managers to accept the benchmark's payoff pattern within the portfolio. In most cases, however, that is not what clients really should want. CMOs are especially valuable for altering the payoff pattern of a mortgage portfolio. In particular, by giving up some of the returns in the unchanged and less-volatile interest rate environments, the portfolio will be better protected from the more extreme outcomes.

Valuation Fundamentals

Investors operate at their own peril if they do not use models as a fundamental building block in the valuation of CMOs. The use of judgment in addition to the model is crucial, but judgment alone is not sufficient. The role of a model is to simplify the valuation problem in order to focus attention on the most important aspects of the problem and to help managers refine their intuition about the security's characteristics and value. A primary advantage of a model is that it provides a consistent framework for sensitivity analysis and for the evaluation of alternative investment opportunities. Of course, to use a model wisely it is necessary to evaluate the effect of altering its key assumptions on the valuation and characteristics of the security.

A few other principles that should guide the valuation process are as follows:
- Begin with the assumption that market prices are fair. This does not mean that finding a cheap security is impossible, but a much wiser initial assumption is that the market is right.

This forces one to critically examine any analysis that suggests a security is cheap.

- Complicated securities can be dissected into pieces that are easier to evaluate.
- A security's risk is equal to its contribution to portfolio risk.
- Yields are not reliable indicators of value. They are almost totally useless for the valuation of mortgage-backed securities.

There is an old saying that "a fool and his money are soon parted." This certainly applies to people who base investment decisions on yields. Indeed, securities can be designed to have high yields and low value. The only reason for looking at yields is to gain historical perspective. Because a long history of option-adjusted spreads (OASs) is not available, examining past yield relationships provides some sense of historical valuation relationships.

The Portfolio Construction Process

The goal of portfolio management is to purchase the cheapest portfolio that has the desired risk and return characteristics. Typically, the desired portfolio has less call risk than the mortgage index, unless mortgages are so cheap that the expected return for bearing the option risk is exceptionally high. The basic approach is to use valuation models combined with sensitivity analysis and considerable judgment. Although much of the analysis is based on OASs, there are many other outputs from valuation models that should be used in conjunction with OASs. In particular, the option-adjusted duration and convexity are used to evaluate the interest rate sensitivity of the security's price. It is also important to evaluate the dollar value of the OAS and the sensitivity of the price to changes in model inputs such as volatility, prepayments, and the shape of the yield curve.

Initial Screen

The process of constructing a portfolio begins with screening the universe for the most attractive types of securities. An optimizer is not useful for this initial screening process because the available optimizers are not sophisticated enough to handle CMOs, but one can mimic an optimization process by following three steps: (1) maximize the OAS subject to a stated portfolio duration, (2) evaluate the portfolio's risk/return characteristics, and (3) revise the portfolio to improve its risk/return characteristics. At this stage, the portfolios to be optimized are composed of a few representative types of securities. For example, one might begin with a discount, current coupon, and premium Fannie Mae mortgage-backed security, some PACs with different average lives, an

IO and a PO, a floater and an inverse floater, and a few support bonds.

The first step in the optimization process is to maximize the OAS, subject to a duration constraint. In theory, duration (option-adjusted interest rate sensitivity of the price) is not a constraint to the extent that futures can be used to offset interest rate risk, but many clients' guidelines limit the ability to use futures. A simple way to start is to plot the OAS as a function of duration for a variety of different types of securities. Barbells and bullets can then be compared to construct the highest OAS portfolio at every level of duration. The trade-off between OAS and duration can be evaluated by computing the ratio of OAS to duration, which is similar to the excess expected return per unit of risk. So, when the ratio is increasing with increases in duration, longer duration portfolios are relatively more attractive, holding other factors constant.

Duration is an incomplete measure of interest rate risk. In part, this is because it ignores changes in the shape of the yield curve and because short rates are more volatile than long rates. In addition, interest rate risk is not the only risk of a mortgage portfolio. So, the next step is to evaluate the portfolio's other risk/return characteristics. For CMOs, this requires calculating the rate of return profile and the time distribution of the cash flows, and evaluating the sensitivity of the OAS and the return and cash flow profiles to the shape of the yield curve, the prepayment expectations, volatility, mortgage spreads, and credit risk. For example, a PAC bond with the same duration as a current coupon mortgage is less sensitive than the mortgage to prepayments, volatility, and mortgage spreads, but it is more sensitive to some changes in the shape of the yield curve. Indeed, different types of securities can have very different payoff patterns and risk characteristics, even if they have the same OAS and duration.

An extremely important aspect of evaluating CMOs is to investigate the time distribution of the cash flows under various prepayment assumptions. For example, it is easy to see how all the pieces of a CMO interact by plotting the cash flows as a function of time for each tranche in the CMO under a variety of prepayment assumptions. Some of the risk inherent in these securities, however, will not be detected if they are investigated only under constant prepayment rates. For example, consider a period of slow prepayments followed by very fast prepayments, and then slow prepayments again. The sensitivity of the return and cash flow profiles to changes in the economic environment not considered in the OAS analysis is another very important consideration. For example, prepayment models, a basic input to mortgage valuation models, are based on historical prepayment experience, but future experience may differ from past experience. So it is important to think about how the time period used for estimation of the model might differ from the future and then investigate the effect of those differences on prepayment patterns and OAS.

The risk/return characteristics of the portfolio should be reevaluated and revised until unwanted bets have been eliminated and the desired payoff pattern achieved. By evaluating the sensitivity of the portfolio's OAS to changes in risk, the most handsomely rewarded risks can be identified. Unfortunately, no well-established equilibrium models have the complexity needed to determine what the market price of these risks should be. The best one can do is to identify what the portfolio risks are and determine which of them offer the highest risk premiums in order to decide how much of each risk should be included in the portfolio.

Detailed Analysis of Securities

Once the most attractive types of securities and the basic portfolio structure have been identified, individual securities must be analyzed in detail. Much of this analysis is designed to check that the OAS is providing an accurate indication of value. The first step is to evaluate the attractiveness of the underlying collateral. If the underlying collateral is not attractive, then it is less likely that a piece of the CMO is cheap. Next, each tranche of the CMO must be evaluated, because if there is a cheap tranche, there must also be an expensive one. It should be possible to identify the expensive part and understand why it is expensive; otherwise it is not likely that a cheap piece has actually been identified. It is also important to evaluate the sensitivity of each tranche to different assumptions, especially regarding prepayments.

Purchasing a tranche of a CMO is equivalent to buying the collateral and selling the other tranches. One useful technique for analyzing a tranche of a CMO is to assume that the collateral is being purchased and financed by the other tranches in the CMO. If selling the other tranches to finance the purchase of the underlying collateral is not attractive, then neither is the tranche being considered for purchase. A by-product of this analysis is an estimate of the dealer's break-even price for the tranche. Knowing the lowest price at which the tranche can be sold is useful for fine-tuning one's bargaining strategy. Approaching the valuation problem from a variety of different directions allows one to hone in on where, if any, the real value is in the structure.

For a variety of reasons, two securities with the same OAS may be cheap by different dollar amounts. OAS assumes that all securities are as liquid as Treasuries and have no credit risk. Also, the change in price for a 1 basis point change in OAS varies across different types of securities. Therefore, it is necessary to evaluate how cheap a security is in dollars. To accomplish this, securities can be dissected into pieces that are easier to evaluate. The theoretical or model value of a bond is equal to the value of default-free and option-free cash flows, plus the value of options purchased, minus the value of options sold, minus the value of credit risk, minus the value of illiquidity. Another method for computing the model value of the security is to determine the OAS that represents fair value for the security, so that the model can be used to compute the price at the fair OAS. For example, the fair OAS should be higher for an esoteric, illiquid CMO than for a PAC bond in a simple CMO structure. The dollar difference between the fair OAS price of a security and its market price is a better method of evaluating its attractiveness than the OAS, analogous to net present value being a better tool than the internal rate of return for capital budgeting.

Simple Tools for Evaluating CMOs

In many cases it is possible to use relatively simple tools to obtain a very close approximation to the OAS of a CMO. The OAS is an expected or average spread over the entire Treasury forward rate curve. With continuous compounding, the spread over the forward rate curve is equivalent to the spread over the zero coupon or spot rate curve. The zero coupon yield for a particular maturity date is the appropriate discount rate for computing the present value of a single default-free and option-free cash flow that is certain to be received on that date. One of the inputs to an OAS model is a fitted zero coupon curve that is derived from the prices of Treasury coupon bonds. This ensures that the OAS model will price Treasury coupon bonds at values very close to their actual market prices. Thus, Treasury coupon bonds are the benchmark for evaluating securities within an OAS framework.

The fitted zero coupon rates can be used to compute the option-free value of the CMO cash flows. Given a base-case prepayment assumption, CMO cash flows can be generated. These cash flows can be discounted to present values using the fitted zero coupon yields to obtain the option-free value of the cash flows. The difference between the option-free value and the market price can be converted to the static spread over the curve by adding a constant spread to each of the zero coupon rates and discounting the cash flows to the present. The spread that causes the present value of the cash flows to equal the market price of the CMO is called the static spread.

The option-adjusted spread is equal to the static spread minus the option cost. Of course, with zero interest rate volatility, the option cost is zero, so the static spread is the OAS with zero volatility. Thus, the static spread is a key component of the OAS, and, therefore, it is often possible to obtain a close approximation to the OAS of a CMO by separately estimating its static spread and option cost.

An approximation of the option cost of a CMO tranche can be derived by allocating the option cost of the underlying collateral across each of the tranches in the CMO. For example, consider how the option cost of the underlying collateral is allocated in a structure that contains PAC bonds, where W is equal to the fraction of the CMO principal allocated to all of the PACs. Then,

$$\text{Collateral Option Cost} = W \times (\text{PAC Option Cost}) + (1-W) \times (\text{PAC Support Option Cost}).$$

This formula is designed to be intuitive. It is not exact because option costs are not rates of return and because the weights (i.e., W) are face-value, not market-value weights. This relationship can be used, for example, to solve for the option cost of a PAC support bond, given the option cost of the underlying collateral and the option cost of the PAC bonds. Specifically,

$$\text{PAC Support Option Costs} = \text{Collateral Option Cost} \div (1-W) - W \times (\text{PAC Option Cost}) \div (1-W).$$

So, for example, if PACs represent 50 percent of the deal (i.e., W is equal to 50 percent), the PAC option cost is 10 basis points, and the collateral option cost is 45 basis points, then the equation above can be used to compute the PAC support option cost of 80 basis points. This is a particularly useful tool because it is relatively easy to estimate the option cost of a PAC and because the option cost of the collateral is available on the daily quote sheets provided by many Wall Street firms. The estimate of the option cost for the entire support class may be allocated across each of the individual tranches in the support class, and likewise for the PAC tranches. The OAS of each tranche may then be estimated by subtracting the option cost of each tranche from its static spread.

Most CMOs are quoted in terms of the yield spread at their weighted average life (WAL), which is the difference between the CMO's yield and the yield of the on-the-run or current coupon Treasury with a maturity close to the WAL of the CMO. Another reason for investigating the zero coupon curve is because it is difficult to determine whether a spread at the WAL is attractive. **Figure 1** shows current coupon Treasuries, fitted zero coupons, and annuity yields as of September 28, 1990. The annuity yields, which are derived from the fitted zero coupon yields, are the appropriate discount rates for computing the present value of a level stream of cash flows. For example, the annuity yields can be used to discount the coupons from a Treasury bond, and the fitted zero coupon yield would be used to compute the present value of the principal payment at maturity. From Figure 1 it is clear that bonds with the same maturity, but with different cash flow patterns, can have very different appropriate discount rates when the Treasury curve is not flat. Thus, it is important to adjust for the effect of the shape of the curve on the value of the future cash flows. The static spread properly adjusts for the shape of the curve because it is a spread over the entire zero coupon curve.

Figure 2 shows the static spread over the zero coupon yield curve and the WAL spread for a CMO with a WAL of seven years. The dot at the top of the WAL spread is the CMO's yield of 9.8 percent, and the dot at the bottom of the WAL spread is the 8.69 percent yield of the seven-year on-the-run Treasury, so the WAL spread is 111 basis points. Based on the WAL spread, the CMO appears to have a wide spread, but its static spread is only 80 basis points.

Figure 1. Current Coupon Treasuries, Fitted Zero-Coupon Yields, and Annuity Yields (9/28/90)

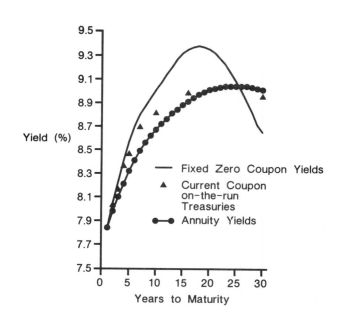

Source: Goldman, Sachs & Co.

Figure 2. Static Spread Versus Weighted-Average Life Spread

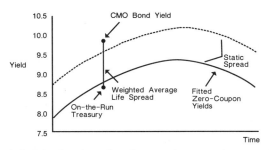

Static Spread = Spread over the entire curve at an assumed prepayment speed
Optional Cost = Static Spread – Option Adjusted Spread

Source: Miller, Anderson & Sherrerd

The WAL spread needs to be adjusted for several factors. Typically, the yields of on-the-run Treasuries are 8 to 10 basis points lower than the yields derived from the fitted zero coupon yields. Therefore, the WAL spread of 111 would be reduced by 10 basis points to 101 basis points. The remaining 21-basis-points difference from the static spread is the result of the shape of the curve. If the CMO is a seven-year PAC bond, for example, the option cost might range from 5 to 10 basis points. So, the magnitude of the option cost of the PAC is much less than the effect of evaluating its yield spread at its weighted-average life instead of looking at its static spread over the entire zero coupon yield curve.

An Example of a Bond Pricing Problem

Pricing bonds can be tricky, as illustrated in the following example. **Table 1** contains some statistics on a cumulative sticky jump-Z bond. A jump-Z bond is an accrual, or Z bond, that jumps ahead of other support tranches in a CMO in terms of the priority of its claim to principal payments when a certain condition, called a trigger, is met. With a cumulative jump-Z, the trigger condition is met only if prepayments since issuance, or cumulatively, exceed a specified prepayment speed. If the jump-Z is sticky, then once it jumps, it always has priority ahead of the bonds it jumped over, even if prepayments subsequently drop below the trigger level. Jump-Z bonds are not an important type of bond, but an analysis of this bond provides a good example of the considerations required when using OAS to evaluate complicated CMOs.

The jump-Z illustrated in Table 1 has a jump trigger at a prepayment speed of 160 PSA (Public Securities Association standard prepayment model). Thus, when prepayments since issuance are greater than 160 PSA, the bond jumps and starts paying down immediately. Reviewing Table 1, consider the dollar price of $93, which is the price the dealer was asking for this bond. At 161 PSA the bond jumps and the yield is 26.8 percent, whereas at 160 PSA it does not jump, and its yield is only 10 percent. If the bond jumps, its first payment is in 0.1 years and it is completely retired in 0.7 years. If it does not jump, the first payment is no sooner than 16.5 years and the final payment is in 29.5 years. Clearly, the value of this bond is very sensitive to prepayments.

This newly issued security was being evaluated during the summer, when prepayments are seasonally high. The underlying collateral was projected to prepay faster than 160 PSA for the next three months, so, according to the model, the bond was definitely going to jump. Prepayment rates for the next few months do not depend on future changes in interest rates because of the time required to process prepayments and because of the standard delay in passing prepayments through to security holders. Thus, for each of the thousands of interest rate scenarios considered by the valuation model, the bond always jumped and, on average, prepaid completely in about 9 months. The OAS was 1900 basis points at a price of $93. Basically, to the model this security looks like a portfolio of one- to nine-month Treasury bills with a 26.8 percent yield. The six-month Treasury-bill yield

Table 1. Bond Pricing Example: Cumulative Sticky Jump-Z Bond

		Yield Table			
		Prepayment Speed (% PSA)			
	0	100	160	161	250
Price					
84	10.3%	10.4%	10.5%	57.0%	70.2%
88	10.1	10.2	10.3	42.6	51.5
93	9.9	9.9	10.0	26.8	31.2
Average Life	28.0	25.0	22.0	0.4	0.3
First Payment	26.3	20.7	16.5	0.1	0.1
Last Payment	29.5	29.5	29.5	0.7	0.5

		Treasury Yields (%)			
6 Mo.	2 Yr.	5 Yr.	10 Yr.	20 Yr.	30 Yr.
7.8	8.07	8.45	8.79	8.98	8.93

Six-month Treasury-bill price: $96.30

Source: Miller, Anderson & Sherrerd

was 7.8 percent, so the OAS equalled about 19 percent, or 1900 basis points. At a price of $97.50, this jump-Z would have an OAS of zero. So, 1900 OAS is worth $97.50 minus $93, or $4.50, which is approximately the same as the dollar value of 100 OAS on a current coupon mortgage. Hence, even though the OAS is large, because it is not earned for very long, it is not worth very much.

Now, having established an understanding of how the OAS model views the security and why it finds the security attractive, it is necessary to evaluate the extent to which the analysis is sensitive to the model's assumptions. Unfortunately, the OAS is misleading in this case. This does not mean that the model is not useful, but it points to the importance of evaluating how changes in the model's assumptions affect the OAS. One issue is that the seasonality of the prepayment function is less relevant for newly issued mortgages, such as those backing this jump-Z, than for seasoned ones. Thus, the prepayment model is causing the probability of jumping to be overstated. Also, prepayments were cyclically low as a result of the weak housing market, a factor not considered by the prepayment model. Based on these considerations it seemed unlikely that prepayments would exceed 160 PSA in the near future.

If the security does not jump soon, however, it is less likely to jump later because after a period of slow prepayments it must prepay much faster than 160 PSA in order to raise the cumulative prepayment speed above 160 PSA. So, if the security does not jump soon, it will effectively become a standard Z-bond with a small probability of jumping. As a standard Z-bond, it could be sold for no more than $83, and the small possibility of jumping in the future is worth less than $2, so if it does not jump in the first month or two, its price will decline to less than $85. If it jumps, its price would increase to no more than $97.50, because after jumping it would not yield less than the 7.8 percent yield on a six-month Treasury bill. Therefore, at a price of $93, the security is negatively convex because its upside is less than $4.50, and its downside is at least $8. Clearly, at $93 this jump-Z is very expensive. These are the types of questions that need to be considered in evaluating the OAS of complicated securities.

The inclusion of a jump-Z in a CMO can have an important effect on the value of other bonds in the structure. This is especially true for the support bonds that are jumped over if its trigger condition is met. Although a jump-Z is itself a support bond, in some cases it can affect the cash flows of the PAC bonds in the structure. This occurs if the accretion from the jump-Z is used to determine the PAC bands (i.e., the range of constant prepayment speeds for which the cash flow schedules of the PAC bonds will be met). Because the Z-bonds are accrual bonds, interest cash flows are available to pay down other tranches in the deal, as long as the Z-bond is accruing interest. If the accretion from a jump-Z is used to increase the range of the PAC bands, however, the range will decrease if a jump occurs. Therefore, PAC bonds in a structure that contains a jump-Z should trade at a concession to PACs from a standard CMO structure.

Conclusion

Derivative mortgage-backed securities offer investors the opportunity to create portfolios with customized payoff patterns. They are especially useful for constructing portfolios with less call and prepayment risk than generic mortgage-backed securities. For example, it is often possible to use derivative mortgage-backed securities to construct portfolios that replicate the cash flows of Treasury securities and cost less than Treasuries. The risks of some of these securities can be large and difficult to identify, especially if they are analyzed using traditional bond-evaluation tools such as yield spreads. Therefore, the use of modern option-based models is an essential part of the process for valuing derivative mortgage-backed securities and for using them to build portfolios.

Question and Answer Session

Question: You have described the use of many models. Do you use proprietary models or are the models you described available to the public?

Dunn: We use Wall Street models rather than developing our own in-house models. Although it would be relatively easy for us to develop an option model, the problem is that for mortgages, a prepayment model is required, and, among other things, this requires maintaining an extensive data base. Also, we find no competitive advantage in trying to develop a prepayment model that is better than what Scott Richard is developing at Goldman, for example. We can add the most value by understanding how the Wall Street models work and by trying to understand the strengths and limitations of the models so that we can use them wisely. We do not want to walk into the future looking backward. By relying on Wall Street to focus on the details, we can focus on the big picture. For example, whenever we are offered a security, we ask for its OAS, and we might also ask that the prepayment function be changed in a certain way to help us evaluate the sensitivity of the security to a change in prepayment behavior.

Question: You did not specifically discuss senior/subordinated deals. For them isn't it possible for the collateral value to be greater than the value of the pieces when the securities are issued?

Dunn: I believe the collateral value is less than the total price of the pieces if you throw in all the pieces, including the subordinated piece and any excess servicing. Indeed, no one would be willing to sell all of the pieces for a total price less than the cost of the collateral.

Question: Do any pension plans use fixed-income managers that only invest in CMOs? If so, what type of plan uses CMO managers?

Dunn: I am not aware of anyone who is exclusively a CMO manager. That is not to say that they do not exist. I do not believe it would be optimal for any type of investor to limit themselves only to CMOs; they are a tool to use in conjunction with other types of securities.

Question: Do you find major differences between the abilities to calculate OAS and other valuation techniques across major Wall Street firms?

Dunn: The major differences tend to be in the prepayment models. It is important to understand what the differences are and to make your own judgments about which ones to believe. It is useful to investigate how the models of a number of different firms value similar securities.

Question: Do you have direct access to some of the models so that if you are offered a security from one firm you could use models from other firms to value it?

Dunn: If one firm is structuring a deal, asking another firm to run it on their model is inappropriate. By using relatively simple tools, however, it is possible to figure out on your own what the OAS would be on another firm's model. One important tool is the static spread over the curve. I will ask to see the cash flows for each tranche in the deal under a variety of different prepayment assumptions. Then, those cash flows can be priced according to the Treasury curve. Also, because I have looked at a number of deals in several models that I trust and understand, I can closely approximate the option cost by examining the cash flows and the nature of the interaction of and priority of the tranches in the deal. After becoming familiar with CMOs, you do not need an OAS run on every bond, because you can dissect a new bond into pieces that you have looked at before.

Valuation Challenges: Asset-Backed/ Swap Securities Markets

James V. Dillon[1]
Vice President
Security Pacific National Bank

The asset-backed securities market began as an outgrowth of the mortgage market to provide alternative liquidity to an originator. It has since developed into a bulk-funding instrument for large and small portfolios of consumer debts such as credit cards and automobile loans. In this presentation, I will discuss the creation of synthetic floating-rate securities by combining an asset-backed security with a swap. For readers who are not active in the swap market, this discussion could be of interest for two reasons: (1) the linkages and relationships within the swap and asset-backed markets might drive spreads, and (2) the mirror-image application—creation of a longer duration security—may be possible by combining a swap with a floating-rate asset.

Development of the Asset-backed and Swap Securities Market

Interest rate swaps started as a credit arbitrage for lower investment-grade issuers and have developed into a flexible tool for managing interest rate risk. Initially, they were brokered transactions between AAA-rated banks and BAA-rated corporations. They have now become hedged transactions, and the two counterparts need not be matched precisely. Creditworthiness is still important, but it is not reflected very much in the swap spreads you may pay.

The asset-backed securities and swap markets grew closer with the advent of controlled amortization and bullet asset-backed securities structures, which reduced the prepayment uncertainty of asset-backed securities and, therefore, reduced the risk of an overswapped position.[2] Some private-market transactions explicitly recognized the linkage between the two markets. For example, some private-placement asset-backed securities transactions have an auction-pricing fall-back provision based on whatever the swap rate might be at that time. Generally, the combination of swaps and asset-backed securities has avoided the problems associated with the risk-controlled arbitrage, which typically combined a long position in a mortgage-backed security with a swap. Risk-controlled arbitrages grew out of the perceived desirability of thrifts to reduce the duration of fixed-rate mortgage-backed securities assets to match the typically short duration of thrift liabilities, a particularly difficult process in a volatile interest rate environment.

The swaps and asset-backed markets grew up together, but separated during the 1980s. Early attempts at finding crossovers have been hampered by the experience many investors had with risk-controlled arbitrage transactions involving fixed-rate mortgage loans. In particular, many investors got burned when premium mortgages were prepaid, leaving them with massive overswapped positions. Using swaps to fund asset-backed securities investments is proving to be less risky and provides more stable returns than risk-controlled arbitrages using mortgages. Some investors now use swaps and caps for thinly capitalized entities such as commercial paper, trusts, and special-purpose corporations that invest in credit card and other asset-backed securities. Some issuers are creating those trusts and special-purpose corporations to off-load assets and sell commercial paper, or they are explicitly pricing their fixed-rate assets based on a swap rate.

The primary advantages of using asset-backed rather than mortgage-backed securities to create an arbitrage are that (1) asset-backed securities are substantially more stable and have more predictable cash flows than mortgage-backed securities; (2) their expected average life is generally shorter, thus reducing risk; (3) their credit spreads are generally wider for the rated risk than medium-term notes of similar maturi-

---

[1] Mr. Dillon substituted for his colleague, Robert J. Kent, who wrote this presentation.

[2] An overswapped position occurs when a mortgage-backed security prepays rapidly, leaving the investor obligated to pay a high fixed rate on the swap while the interest earned on the mortgage-backed security is significantly reduced.

ty and quality, and (4) they permit synthetic realization of relative value between fixed- and floating-rate markets.

Generic swaps are quoted as a spread to current U.S. Treasury securities, usually on a semiannual bond basis versus a three- or six-month LIBOR (London Interbank Offered Rate). Quotes are given for a 2-, 3-, 4-, 5-, 7-, or 10-year swap beginning two business days from execution day. Bullet swaps for maturities other than these are typically quoted as a curvilinear interpolation of the adjacent on-the-run swap rates. Monthly amortizing swaps are quoted at a fixed rate versus one-month LIBOR based on an assumed principal amortization schedule. The swap rate is a weighted average of a blended series of individual swaps.

Asset-backed securities are quoted at a semiannual equivalent spread to the U.S. Treasury security with an equivalent average life (in the case of an amortizing asset-backed security), or final maturity (in the case of a bullet-maturity asset-backed security). The usual delay period from the accrual date of an asset-backed security to the payment date for final maturity is 15 days—in mortgage terminology, a "45-day stated delay," but conventionally referred to as a "15-day delay."

One of the standard formulas for converting monthly pay to semiannual pay, with or without a delay period, is shown in **Exhibit 1**.

Other issues must also be considered in combining a swap with an asset-backed security. As in any transaction, the compounding basis and the day-count convention basis should be the same for each type of security, but also the accrual periods and payment dates should also match. The nominal yield of a deal with a payment delay will differ greatly from the realized yield, unless the impact of the delay is reflected in the swap. Other issues, such as the treatment of a payment date that falls on a weekend, are also important.

As the swap market has grown in sophistication,

its ability to accommodate more unusual structures presented by asset-backed securities deals has increased commensurately. Swaps can be quoted according to any payment frequency or day-count convention, adjusted for short or long first-payment periods, quoted for forward settlement, or quoted for off-market coupons.

Requirements for Successful Asset-backed Security/Swap Transactions

The requirements for successful asset-backed security/swap transactions are (1) swapped yields that equal or exceed the targeted all-in yield, (2) liquid markets for both swaps and asset-backed securities, (3) predictable cash flow to avoid over- or underswapped positions, and (4) creditworthy counterparties for swaps and solid issuers for asset-backed securities.

For individual investors at selected maturities, the ability to enter into a swap transaction meeting the targeted net yield will depend on the supply of issues in the selected range. All other things being equal, the current market offers a wider than normal swap spread. Although a swap market can be thought of as a generic market with respect to counterparty credit risk, this has not been the case for the asset-backed securities market.

Figure 1 shows a two- to four-year composite of credit card and swap spreads from January 1987 to March 1990. The spread difference has widened significantly in recent months. Current swap spreads on the offer side range from about 53 basis points over two-year Treasuries to about 65 basis points over five-year Treasuries. Swaps of three years and under are priced off of the Eurodollar futures market; swaps with maturities greater than three years are priced off the Treasury market. Some fairly attractive synthetic floating-rate securities (synthetic floaters) can be created at quite a wide spread over LIBOR. Note that although the asset-backed securities spreads have historically been wider than swap spreads, they have also been much more volatile, which has allowed the asset-backed security/swap transaction to work.

For the asset-backed security/swap to succeed, the net spread must meet the investor's targeted spread, which for banks currently is about 10 to 40 basis points depending on their funding costs. Bank funding costs are rising now, so for a bank to do this transaction and create a synthetic floater, a much wider spread is needed now than at this time last year. This may be one of the factors allowing the spreads on asset-backed securities to rise. The need for a wider spread could also explain why less arbitrage is occurring today as compared with last year. Asset-backed

---

Exhibit 1. All-in Amortizing Swap Rate Quoted on a Monthly, Money Market Basis

1. Swap rate = 0.0917 monthly, money market

2. $(1 + \frac{0.0917}{12})^{12} = (1 + \frac{X}{2})^2$

$$X = [(1 + \frac{0.917}{12})^6 - 1] \times 2$$

$$X = 9.35\%$$

3. $9.35\% \times \frac{365}{360} = 9.48\%$ Semi-bond basis

Source: Security Pacific National Bank

Figure 1. Credit Card Versus Swap Spreads (Two-Year Average Life)

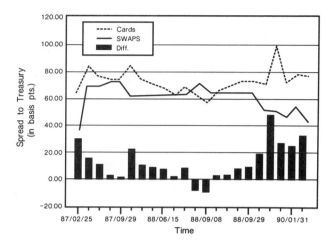

Source: Security Pacific National Bank

securities offer the only investment-grade security for which a positive LIBOR swap spread is generally available. For example, pure AAA-rated issuers generally sell medium-term notes at 10 to 20 basis points below LIBOR. During the past few years, asset-backed security spreads have tended to widen in the fourth quarter, when the largest volume of new issuance generally occurs.

Figure 2 illustrates swap spreads from 1987 to 1990. It was constructed using a generic two-year swap spread for automobile loan asset-backed securities. The swap spread for these has generally been wider on average than that for credit cards. Credit card asset-backed securities have all been issued by AAA-rated issuers, whereas the automobile asset-backed securities market includes a mix of AAA-rated and AA-rated issuers, which provides some explanation for the wider spreads for automobile asset-backed securities.

Asset-backed Securities/Swap Liquidity

Liquidity plays a vital role in all financial markets, but particularly in synthetics, for which two or more transactions are entered into to achieve a desired investment result. As the swap market developed with bank and nonbank participants, the gross position, or total notional amount, on institutions' swap books

grew. For many dealer banks, the gross level of swaps outstanding is larger than their total assets. Larger swap participants use more sophisticated hedging techniques than just entering into exactly matching counterswaps. These techniques have greatly improved the availability of amortizing and custom-tailored swaps that meet the requirements of individual transactions. Swaps can be quoted on a 30/360-day basis and 15 days forward to match typical asset-backed security structures. Bid-ask spreads for a generic swap are 4 to 5 basis points in the two- to five-year range for U.S. dollar swaps. As swaps become more customized, however, liquidity may be slightly reduced and spreads may increase.

Issuers of asset-backed securities generally do not quote swaps to guarantee a perfect match for their own amortizing asset-backed securities transactions because of the risk that sale treatment would be jeopardized. With bullet-type structures, however, it may be possible to enter into a generic swap that matches the expected pay dates for a particular asset-backed securities transaction.

Since 1985, the growth in the asset-backed market and the development of more bondlike asset-backed securities structures have led to a fairly active secondary market for asset-backed securities. Currently, asset-backed securities can be purchased with maturities from six months to 10 years. One risk to the liquidity of the asset-backed securities market is that

Figure 2. Automobile Versus Swap Spreads (Two-Year Average Life)

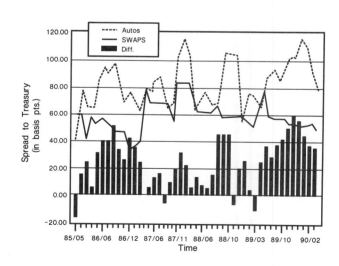

Source: Security Pacific National Bank

these issues tend to be as large as $4 billion, so issuers may have some difficulty readily refinancing a bullet maturity in this market.

The Need for Stable Cash Flows

Taken as individual transactions, many amortizing asset-backed securities transactions have missed their expected cash flows by substantial amounts, and when this happens they are either "fast pay" or "slow pay." By the end of six months to one year, a given pool may be one or the other, but it seldom fluctuates. During their first two or so years of life, portfolio transactions—pools made of a random selection of a lender's entire portfolio—tend to miss their expected payment speeds by less than single-month-originated transactions do; for example, the GMAC pools have had both fast-pay and slow-pay margins substantially wider than the market as a whole. After the early years of their lives, the pool payment speeds diverge from the model results by larger margins than the single-month-origination transactions.

Part of the reason for this apparently random behavior of pools is that single-loan models are the ones most frequently used to generate projected cash flows. These models treat the pool as a single loan, using the pool's weighted-average interest rate, weighted-average maturity, and a standard prepayment formula based on whether an absolute or conditional prepayment rate was used. Investors who analyze an amortizing pool of loans based on single-loan model cash flows provided at the inception of a pool generally believe a pool slows down as it ages, because the longer-maturity loans in a pool were not accounted for in the single-pool analysis. We call this a weighted-average maturity (WAM) drift.

Figure 3 shows the effect of WAM drift on a pool of automobile loans originated by Security Pacific between 1985 and February 1987 and then sold in November 1987. The problem is not with the performance of the pool, but with the point-of-sale measurement system, which does not account for WAM drift. In a more perfect world, the investor in a given pool would be provided a portfolio tape from which a cash flow schedule could be generated at the point of sale and updated monthly. Unfortunately, most active investors in asset-backed securities have neither the capability nor the cost structure to support this level of analysis. Only slightly less perfect is the computer-generated cash flow forecast delivered at point of sale that incorporates the expected WAM drift. Security Pacific generated this type of schedule in 1987, in part to satisfy tax counsel, which saw the difference between the 15.65 coupon and the 8.20 pass-through rate

Figure 3. Security Pacific 87-B Grantor Trust WAM Drift

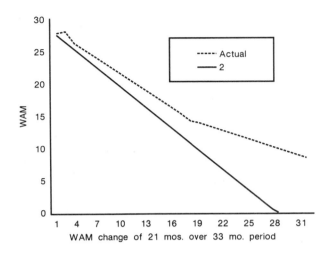

Source: Security Pacific National Bank

as a stripped bond.

As **Figure 4** shows, the Security Pacific cash flow projection significantly improved upon the single-loan model projection in forecasting the actual cash flow from the pool. Using this kind of cash flow model can significantly improve an investor's fore-

Figure 4. Security Pacific 87-B Actual Versus Projected Paydown

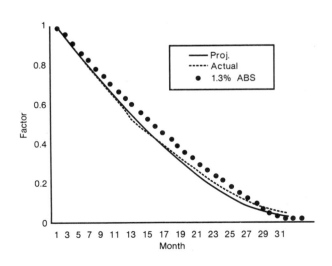

Source: Security Pacific National Bank

casting capability and, therefore, the ability to execute an efficient swap. A swap executed on this cash flow forecast would reduce under- or overswapped positions to an average of less than 1 percent of the expected principal value, compared to about 2 percent under- or overswapped for the single-loan model. In a rapidly rising or falling interest rate environment, this improvement translates into approximately 6 basis points in realized yields.

A second strategy to reduce variance is diversification. Some pools appear to be fast-pay and others slow-pay for the same issuer. Diversification of asset-backed securities transactions can reduce this variance using only four or five amortizing asset-backed securities transactions. **Figure 5** compares the pool factors with expected values for 57 automobile loan transactions outstanding at March 31, 1990. Any conditional prepayment rates used at pricing were converted to an approximate asset-backed securities equivalent. The mean difference from expected values was 0.76 percent of the original principal amount, with a range from -4.7 percent to 11.9 percent. This suggests that diversification would significantly reduce the impact of individual variances.

For credit card-backed securities, the case for stability of cash flow is even greater. Other than Republic Bank of Texas's transactions, in which investors were paid early, I am not aware of any transactions that differ significantly from their expected pool factors over time. This record is testimony to the conservatism of the rating agencies and investment bankers and to the diligence of issuers in servicing and maintaining portfolio quality.

One element of interest for swap participants and fixed-rate investors alike is that the market maintains a substantial spread differential between controlled-amortization, soft-bullet, and hard-bullet transactions, although no risk differential has been demonstrated to date.[3] The spread for controlled-amortization as opposed to soft-bullet transactions has ranged from 5 to 10 basis points; the spread for soft-bullet compared to hard-bullet transactions has been 3 to 5 basis points.

Credit Quality

As noted earlier, asset-backed securities have enjoyed a yield advantage compared to similarly rated medium-term notes and the generic swap market. To some extent, this yield premium reflects the overall decline in

[3]Soft-bullet structures permit shortening or lengthening of final maturities under certain defined events which are typically considered to have a very low probability. Hard-bullet structures do not allow these adjustments.

Figure 5. Automobile Asset-Backed Prepayment Experience

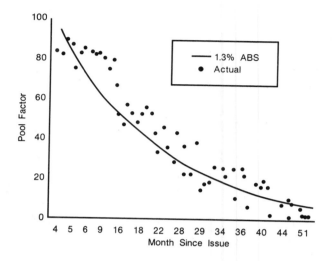

Source: Security Pacific National Bank

creditworthiness of three principal issuers of asset-backed securities: financial institutions, retailers, and automobile finance companies. For swapped asset-backed securities, the credit risk may be increased by counterparty risk on the swap transaction or the costs may be increased by regulatory actions. Rating agencies have issued ratings based on legal opinions that transactions are bankruptcy-remote.

Conclusion

During the past five years, the technologies of the asset-backed securities and swap markets have moved together and have fulfilled the requirements for their successful linkage. Fixed-to-floating, internal, and external swaps have been executed with success. Floating-to-fixed swaps are somewhat less common than the fixed-to-floating variety because the volume of floating-rate asset-backed securities is limited. The market does not yet seem to be very efficient, however, as wide fluctuations in net spreads continue to occur. Amortized automobile asset-backed securities have demonstrated cash flow stability worthy of increased activity in this area. Credit card transactions bring an even higher level of predictability but have not yet achieved AAA status in terms of spread. These factors continue to present opportunities for swap-driven investors.

Question and Answer Session

Question: What is the trend in two- to five-year swap spreads during 1990, and how have spreads been affected as the general level of interest rates have declined and the yield curve has steepened?

Dillon: That question goes even beyond the U.S. dollar market. We have seen a great tightening of swap spreads throughout the world, principally in the deutsche mark and yen markets, as well as the U.S. dollar market. To determine what is driving that, we would have to segment the U.S. dollar swap market into two parts. Although the three-years-and-under swaps are quoted over the Treasury rate, they are really priced based on the Eurodollar futures markets— that is, the swap rate is the internal rate of return of a strip of Eurodollar futures. As the TED (Treasury-Eurodollar) spread collapsed in the middle of 1990, swaps spreads narrowed accordingly. Generally, as interest rates decline, the conventional wisdom is that swap spreads rise for supply and demand reasons. As lower rates occur, corporations enter the market to pay fixed, to lock in the perceived low interest rates, driving swap spreads up. We have not seen this demand come into the market from the sideline, which may be some indication that the recessionary effects are deeper than some people might believe (i.e., the fundamental demand for fixed-rate debt may not be as strong as swap market participants expect it to be).

In addition, implied volatility in the caps and floor market has been off dramatically. Some participants cite structural factors and accounting regulations for Japanese banks as explanations.

In any event, a lot of people are making big bets on certain swap spreads widening out, and more bets are being made in the non-U.S. dollar markets than in the U.S. dollar markets.

Question: Please define risk-controlled arbitrage.

Dillon: Risk-controlled arbitrage is not a very popular thing these days, particularly with the thrift regulators in Washington. Basically, a risk-controlled arbitrage is an arbitrage in which someone would buy mortgages at, for example, 11 percent, and swap at 10 percent, thus creating a LIBOR plus 100 synthetic floating-rate asset. Some worked out very well, but the ones that were structured with premium mortgages got burned when the premiums prepaid significantly. When the mortgages prepaid, the thrifts still had to pay 10 percent in the swap but could only reinvest at a lower rate, for example 9 percent. This vehicle was popular among the thrifts back in the mid-1980s. The problem was not necessarily in the concept but in the testing of the sensitivities, such as the changes in the level of rates and the slope of the yield curve.

Question: Given the advent of securitization, are you concerned about doing swaps with financial institutions that now have fewer assets on their books and are thus less diversified?

Dillon: The easy answer is no. For example, we are selectively doing swaps with thrifts now because we think FIRREA (Financial Institutions Reform, Recovery and Enforcement Act) protects us as a swap dealer. To the degree that we have collateral, we feel safe. Swap risk is a complex issue. Unlike buying a Security Pacific medium-term note, no principal exposure is involved in a swap, and the gross interest is not at risk. But we are being more careful. If my credit people are concerned about the impact of asset securitization, they have not relayed that concern to me, and we are still active in the swap market with financial institutions.

The Application of Securitization on Corporate Balance Sheets

Jerald M. Wigdortz
Managing Director
Salomon Brothers Inc

Securitization can be used to help deposit-taking institutions meet a number of objectives. I will discuss how securitization is being used to manage the funding of financial institutions. This application is especially interesting in the current capital market environment.

This technology was developed to securitize investment-grade portfolios of financial assets held by investment-grade financial institutions. Scrutiny by bank regulators of highly leveraged transactions lending, however, combined with the elimination of the junk bond market as a viable capital source for noninvestment-grade corporations, has made the use of securitization technology more interesting to noninvestment-grade companies. There have not been a lot of these transactions yet, but I think there will be.

The Asset-Backed Securities Market

The asset-backed securities market has been growing steadily. **Figure 1** shows the issuance of public asset-backed securities from 1966 through 1990. Historically, the second half of the year has been stronger than the first half in terms of the volume of new issuance. I think 1990 will follow the same pattern. Most of us have been predicting a huge surge in the fourth quarter—something on the order of $10 to $15 billion—given the number of issuers who have either filed or are talking about filing.

Figure 2 shows the distribution of institutions that have issued the most asset-backed securities. Commercial banks and thrifts have done most of the securitization, although retailers, finance companies, and industrial companies have also used this market.

Benefits to Investment-Grade Companies

Securitization offers several benefits to issuers. For investment-grade companies, these include off-balance-sheet financing, increased tax efficiency, and insulation against event risk. Off-balance-sheet financing improves the capital ratios of financial institutions. This may help issuers secure better credit ratings and, consequently, lower financing rates.

Structured transactions are often driven by tax considerations. Leasing is the traditional type of tax-motivated structured financing. For companies with excess foreign tax credits, even more compelling tax incentives exist as a result of interest allocation rules as defined by the IRS. For instance, interest allocation rules prevent using all of the interest expense on U.S. debt to offset income if a company has substantial international operations. Securitization can allow a direct offset. **Table 1** shows that, for a company with a 34 percent tax rate and with 35 percent of its interest deduction allocable to foreign source income, the after-tax effect attributable to securitization is 72 basis points—even though the pretax cost of funds is dramatically different. Today major corporations, including some AAA-rated companies that have large finance subsidiaries, are studying this effect.

Insulation from event risk is another benefit of securitization, although event risk is considered less important in this market than in other markets. During 1990, there was a period when event risk imposed some real penalties in the form of wider spreads.

Benefits to Noninvestment-Grade Companies

For noninvestment-grade companies, there are two benefits of securitization: strategic financing of assets and restructuring existing debt. Noninvestment-grade companies can securitize the high-quality cash flows from trade receivables, inventories, commerical mortgages, and franchise payments. From a strategic perspective, trade receivables should be financed on their own merits as investment-grade securities. If the creditworthiness of those owing the money is higher than that of the firm to which they owe it, it

Figure 1. History of Public Asset-Backed Issuance (1986-1990)

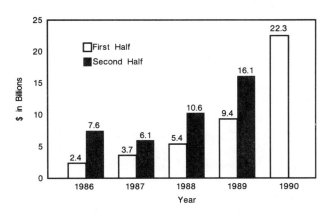

Source: Salomon Brothers Inc

Figure 2. Distribution of Public Asset-Backed Issuance (As of June 30, 1990)

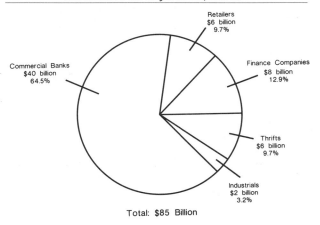

Source: Salomon Brothers Inc

makes sense to use their credit rather than the weaker credit of the noninvestment-grade company to support the security. This can best be done using an off-balance-sheet method such as securitization.

For example, we did a private placement transaction for a Latin American entity that was selling geothermal electric power to investment-grade U.S. utilities under long-term supply contracts. In this case, and many others, it makes more sense to use the receivable's credit rating to obtain financing than to use the originating company's own rating.

Similarly, physical assets with a definable market value—for instance, inventories—may be more efficiently financed by noninvestment-grade companies using securities backed by inventories. Securitization is only more efficient, however, when the inventory consists of hard assets whose market value is easily estimated, for example raw materials or other types of

Table 1. Interest Allocation Benefits of Securitization

	After-Tax Cost of Funds for AAA-rated Corporation	
	Two-Year Securitization	Two-Year Securitization
Pretax cost of funds (T + 0.85 vs. T + 0.45)	8.65%	8.25%
After-tax cost of funds*	5.71%	6.43%
Securitization: Better/(Worse)	0.72%	

* After-tax cost of funds is based on a 34 percent tax rate and the assumption that 35 percent of interest deduction is allocable to foreign source income.

Source: Salomon Brothers Inc

natural resources and, in some cases, cash crops. One must be careful to eliminate inventory that is only valuable to those using it to make a finished product. Securitization is very useful when the inventory can be used easily by many others.

Other high-quality cash flows can be isolated and financed through a structured transaction. For example, consider a company that has business units or parts of units with relatively stable cash flows and low production costs that could be isolated and used to support financing. In these cases we are taking securitization to its high-tech extreme. To the extent that you could find an entity within a corporation with these characteristics, however, it is theoretically possible to envision securitized financing against this stream of very stable cash flows.

Restructuring existing bank debt can often produce significant cost savings for noninvestment-grade companies. Consider a highly leveraged company that has a large chunk of bank debt (senior secured debt) and a sliver of equity. This debt can be restructured at a cost savings to the firm. Furthermore, investment-grade structured financings typically do not impose restrictive financial covenants on the seller.

Table 2 shows a company that has $1 billion of secured bank debt on its books, paying about 360 basis points over the converted Treasury rate. A number of transactions can be done. Given the market rates at the time, the following transactions are possible: a $200 million receivables transaction; a $210 million inventory transaction; a $140 million property, plant, and equipment transaction; and a secured transaction on everything else. Assuming reasonable ratings and spreads, the weighted-average savings for the firm are between 61 and 140 basis points over Treasury.

Table 2. Restructure Existing Debt

Type	Amount (MM)	Implied Rating	Treasury Spread
Bank debt	$1,000	BB–	360 bp
Receivables transaction	200	AAA	95 – 100
Inventory transaction	210	A	105 – 125
PP&E transaction	240	BBB	150 – 200
Secured debt	450	B+	350 – 500
Total Savings			61 – 140

*   Floating-rate bank debt is assumed to be priced at reserve-adjusted LIBOR + 250 basis points (bp) and has been swapped into five-year fixed.

Source: Salomon Brothers Inc

Conclusion

I think securitization will continue to grow. It reduces uncertainty. Rating agencies and investors will be much more confident about properly structured asset-backed transactions than they could possibly be about senior unsecured notes. Once investors become comfortable with these types of transactions, and with the structures used to insulate and isolate the cash flows and assets to support a transaction, they will become more comfortable with them than with regular unsecured senior corporate debt. Buying unsecured senior debt means buying a whole portfolio of businesses within that organization, not just a specific set of cash flows associated with a specific business or group of assets.

Question and Answer Session

Question: In your illustration of the tax efficiency of securitization *vis-à-vis* foreign tax credit, is there an optimal tenor and size for securitization?

Wigdortz: I'm not sure. It depends on the amount of foreign source income, the size of the financing done in the United States, and the U.S. interest expenses. It's not an easy question to answer, but I think an analysis of the question could be done.

Question: Are there new risks associated with restructuring a firm's bank debt, as illustrated in Table 2?

Wigdortz: There are timing and bankruptcy risks in using off-balance-sheet financings.

Question: Are there extra costs associated with servicing the asset-backed securities that a firm would not encounter with bank debt?

Wigdortz: Yes. The biggest cost relates to systems. One must have systems capable of tracking and reporting the cash flows associated with the assets used for a structured financing.

Question: How will an economic recession affect the asset-backed securities market?

Wigdortz: A recession will stress some of the groups of assets used in asset-backed financings. If there are no mishaps during this period of increased concern, it will highlight the positive aspects of this financing technique.

Securitization and Strategic Planning for Banks and Thrifts[1]

Juan M. Ocampo
Principal
McKinsey & Company, Inc.

Most of the presentations in these proceedings discuss securitization from the investor's perspective. Securitization can be used as a strategic tool for banks and thrifts—the originators—as well. It also presents some dangers, however. In this presentation, I will discuss both the limitations and the benefits of securitization from the perspective of banks and thrifts.

Limitations of Securitization

An asset-backed security is only as good as the credit portfolios, or assets, that underlie the security and the credit management process that keeps the security sound. Credit portfolios are subject to both environmental and operational risks. Environmental risk is a measure of the portfolio's sensitivity to external shocks—for example, a recession. Operational risk is independent of the economy at large. The level of operational risk is a function of the skill of the underwriter, particularly with respect to portfolio monitoring.

The attractiveness of an asset for securitization depends on where it falls in the operational-risk/environmental-risk framework. As shown in **Figure 1**, some credit portfolios have higher environmental risk than others. Higher levels of environmental risk are associated with higher levels of potential loss, and thus those portfolios are not suitable for securitization. Figure 1 also shows the relative operational risk of different credit portfolios. The assets with high levels of operational risk also are not suitable for securitization.

Portfolios with low operational risk and low environmental risk—for example, the high-grade corporate money-market loans—are the most attractive types of assets for securitization, and many have been securitized in an unstructured manner for years. Commercial paper and loan syndication markets are examples. Assets whose value is subject to the quality of the monitoring of the originator but which have some insensitivity to environmental cyclicity (low environmental/high operational risk) are the newest frontier for securitization.

The risk of underlying credits changes with time. **Figure 2** illustrates the impact of portfolio aging on credit losses for a portfolio with low environmental and high operational risk. The loss rate of this portfolio tends to peak fairly early. This configuration is most evident in credit card portfolios. As these season, the losses tend to occur at a high level but within a reasonable band. Although the economy affects these types of assets, their overall credit quality is more dependent on the skill of the originator in monitoring the portfolio and eliminating bad credits as they occur.

Highly leveraged transactions, middle-market credits, and real estate construction loans show a different pattern. At first, they have very few losses no matter how bad the economy is; however, the distribution of potential loss increases over time and can wipe out the value of a portfolio. Predicting how this type of portfolio is going to behave is very difficult. The originator sees a very low up-front loss rate, whereas the investor and credit enhancer see the potential for a catastrophe at the end. Because that gap is hard to close, securitization does not work very well for these types of assets.

The limitations of securitization can be illustrated using commercial real estate. The commercial real estate market has been weak for a long time. **Figure 3** shows the U.S. commercial real estate rent-vacancy cycle. The market has had very sharp, pronounced troughs lasting many years, and this pattern is typical of most markets and most cities. Going through a long bull market tends to make people forget how devastating the downward portion of the cycle can be. Down markets tend to catch banks by surprise.

Figure 1. Credit Portfolio Types

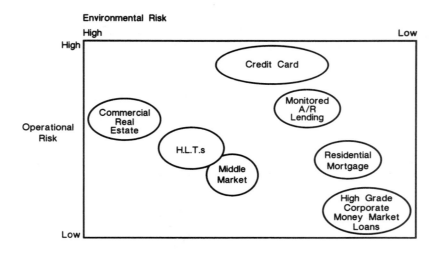

Source: McKinsey & Company, Inc.

The Dallas office market illustrates why real estate loans are not good candidates for securitization. **Figure 4** shows the rent-vacancy cycles of the Dallas office market during the 1980s. According to the trend of effective rents, the market looked attractive between 1980 and 1984. Vacancies had been declining, driving rents up. The trend was changing, how-ever. The early warning signals came as early as 1981 from some of the market professionals in Dallas who believed that, based on the level of construction that was planned but not yet constructed, massive over-capacity was inevitable. Nevertheless, the banks kept lending into this market. The first sign of overheating was when vacancy rates shot up, although effective

Figure 2. Impact of Portfolio Aging on Credit Losses

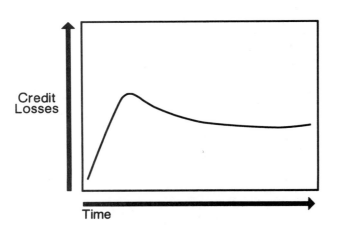

Source: McKinsey & Company, Inc.

Figure 3. Real Estate Rent-Vacancy Cycle (1968-88)

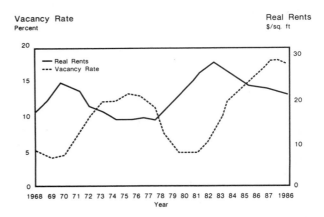

Source: McKinsey & Company, Inc.

Figure 4. Dallas Office Market (1976-88)

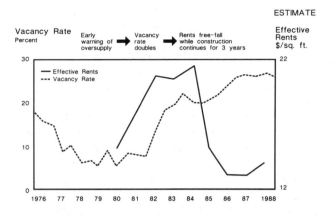

Source: McKinsey & Company, Inc.

rents were still climbing. This happens as people switch to better-quality buildings, and it is always a precursor of a down market. After 1984, rents entered a free-fall, but construction continued for another three years. Much of that construction had been committed to in 1982, 1983, and 1984.

Figure 5 shows what can happen to a commercial real estate loan in a market like Dallas. In this example, the value of the project when the loan is approved is $289 million and its cost is $248 million. Initially, the bank agrees to lend $200 million, and the

developer agrees to put up $48 million of equity. As the market starts to decline, the building takes a lot longer to lease, so the bank must put up more money to carry the property—in this case, another $66 million. Meanwhile, because of changes in the capitalization rates and the expected rental income, the property value has declined to $229 million. Several years later, lease-up costs have continued to consume cash, and the bank is out another $21 million, bringing its total exposure to $287 million. Meanwhile, the building again has lost value because of the discounting of a much lower rental stream. Its value is down to $183 million. What had looked like a very good loan at the beginning has turned into a $100 million loss, assuming no cost overruns or delays in construction itself.

This type of loan is not suitable for creating an asset-backed security. A suitable credit portfolio has more stable collateral and more predictable loss patterns than real estate-backed securities have. The accounts receivable program for a regional bank illustrates how securitization can help the credit problem. **Figure 6** shows the percent of commercial loans that went on nonaccrual at any time, by the company's initial credit ranking. The portfolios show some fairly high losses created by the traditional middle-market and corporate lending officers. Such assets often are secured but not carefully monitored. The portfolios originated by the asset-based lending group show much lower losses, primarily because they were being monitored on a formula basis and because the problems were being worked out before they got too bad. Overall, when such a portfolio is properly run and properly monitored, it can do well.

Figure 5. Real Estate Construction Credit ($ Millions)

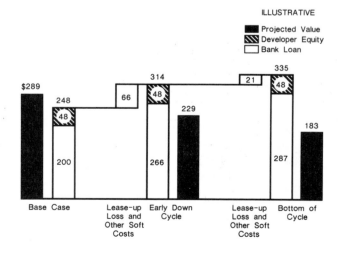

Source: McKinsey & Company, Inc.

Figure 6. Percent of Commercial Loans That Went on Nonaccrual at Any Time (Regional Banking)

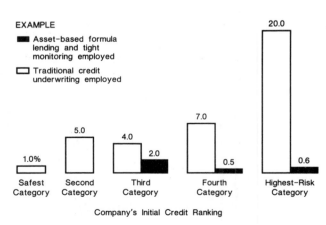

Source: McKinsey & Company, Inc.

Direct Benefits of Securitization

Securitization based on appropriate assets, such as well-managed portfolios of credit cards or other accounts receivable, can offer both direct and indirect benefits to the originators. The direct benefits include improved capital efficiency and enhanced deposit spreads.

The benefits of improved capital lending can be illustrated by using credit card securitization. **Figure 7** shows the incremental contribution of removing assets from the balance sheet through securitization of the accounts receivable. This portfolio has a very high gross yield—16.62 percent. The funding costs are higher for securitization than for traditional operations. The senior servicing fee is not affected by the structure, but both the credit losses and the capital costs are. If credit losses go above a certain amount, the investor or credit enhancers will bear some of the losses in a securitized structure, but this is highly unlikely to happen; thus, I have shown 132 basis points of expected loss for both. The major cost advantage of securitization is lower capital costs. In this case, the savings is about 130 basis points. Because of lower capital requirements, a bank can do more business, as long as it is a securitizable asset with a much lower kind of capital. The net contribution is 350 basis points versus 278 basis points for traditional operations. In this example, for a $500 million portfolio, securitization provides an incremental $3.6 million a year in contribution.

The second direct benefit is repricing of deposits once alternative sources of financing have been found. Most bankers consider their funding costs to be their average costs. They look at their marginal deposit, which tends to be a certificate of deposit (CD), and with some adjustments, they consider the rate paid on that to be their marginal cost of funds. The marginal cost of funds is really much higher, however, although the exact amount depends on the specific situation of the bank, the quality of its branch network, and its natural clientele.

The true marginal deposit cost includes at least two other elements: the incremental yield effect on all CDs, and the cannibalization of lower-cost deposits. Because a bank cannot price-discriminate, to get incremental funding—that is more deposits—it must pay all customers higher rates, not just the new customers. This is extremely expensive. Cannibalization makes the situation worse. The greater the spread between passbook and money market accounts relative to CDs, the greater the probability that the lower-cost deposits will switch to higher-cost deposits. Besides being more expensive, the CDs tend to be of lower duration because they have a fixed maturity rather than a stochastic one. The magnitude of the impact of these two elements depends a great deal on the natural deposit base of the institution, but it could be as much as 30 basis points across the board. This would create a marginal cost of funds in excess of 20 percent.

The problem can be further aggravated by the price elasticities in the deposit markets. **Figure 8** illustrates a deposit rate elasticity curve; the actual curve will vary by location and bank. Price elasticity follows a simple S curve. For instance, if a bank is paying the market rate, it will plot in the middle of the S. To capture more volume, the bank will have to increase its yield relative to other banks. The bank will get very little incremental volume at first because a

Figure 7. Improved Capital Efficiency

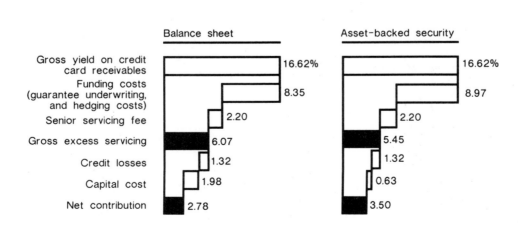

Source: McKinsey & Company, Inc.

market usually has only a small number of price shoppers—people who will shift their funds for relatively small additional amounts of return. To increase its funding base, the bank starts to pay a big premium; it rides the S curve up. By the time the price premium starts to have an impact on volume, the bank is paying a substantial penalty on its cost of funds.

Securitization forces banks to examine their deposit pricing market-by-market. The cost/volume relationship is all relative to the competition in a given market—it will be different in Boston than in Chicago, for example. Securitization can move a bank out of that inefficient market range. The result is a greater net contribution on deposits across the entire structure, achieved with only a modest loss of volume.

The benefits of improved deposit pricing are in addition to the capital efficiencies. Using this analysis to lower the entire average deposit base shrinks the balance sheet but changes nothing in terms of asset price. The result can be another 20 basis points of return on assets for a typical bank.

Indirect Benefits of Securitization

Securitizing assets also offers indirect benefits: the ability to lay off local market risk and achieve a tighter market focus; more efficient functional specialization, which results in accelerated market-share gains and reduced marketing costs; and external credit and pricing scrutiny and enhanced management information. All banks can realize these benefits, not just those that securitize, but they tend to accrue to those that secu-

ritize because of the discipline of the securitization process.

The first indirect benefit comes from greater focus on a specific customer segment or geographic market. The increased attention minimizes the probability that the bank will be exposed to inappropriate portfolio concentrations. This comes as a result of being able to lay off the catastrophe risk in the asset-based structures. **Figure 9** shows an example of risk-sharing for a traditional letter-of-credit deal. The same logic applies for senior subordination. Essentially, the originator absorbs a known amount of loss, perhaps as much as twice the expected loss of the portfolio. If it is a highly analyzable portfolio with considerable stability in its expected losses, with credit enhancers taking eight times and the investor taking the balance, the investors are operating, in effect, as reinsurers. The highly unlikely risk is not borne by the originator but by someone else—in this case, the investors. That becomes relevant in highly concentrated portfolios, because the credit enhancer is actually providing a safety net.

Securitization creates a form of risk-based capital that is implemented by the private markets. **Figure 10** compares costs of securitized lending for a weak credit underwriter and a strong one. The weak one has a 200-basis-point expected loss on its portfolio, and the strong one has a 100-basis-point expected loss. The apparent difference in the cost of lending would be 100 basis points. If you securitize, however, the cost is 143 basis points, because the weak underwriter must keep that much more capital in its spread account. Therefore, the originator, who is bet-

Figure 8. Deposit Rate Elasticities

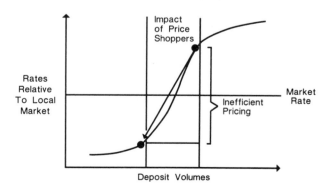

Figure 9. Risk Repackaging Through Credit Enhancement: General Approach for AAA-Rated Structures

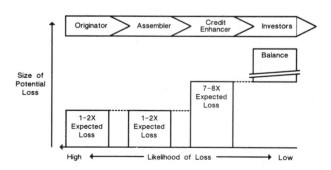

Source: McKinsey & Company, Inc.

Source: McKinsey & Company, Inc.

Figure 10. Cost of Securitized Lending (Basis Points Per Annum)

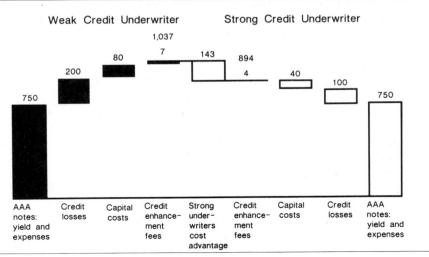

Source: McKinsey & Company, Inc.

ter at credit, has a real advantage.

Throughout the 1990s, there will be a real difference between those who win and those who lose. Basically, winners will get considerably cheaper capital if they have good credit underwriting and monitoring records. In good credit management, lenders who focus on their business will do much better. If a bank can stave off the potential for catastrophe created by being overconcentrated, it can reduce its overall expected loss level.

The second indirect benefit of securitization comes from more efficient functional specialization. Securitization is not a requirement for this, but it tends to be related. A bank can focus on originating and develop better originators and better credit management. Better originators can accelerate market-share gains and obtain some local-scale economies in marketing.

A simple sensitivity analysis shows that if you take an incremental dollar of capital that is generated by retained earnings, you can leverage it up and lend out $15. If the lender securitizes his loan production, and is running at an identifiable and provable 100-basis-point annual charge-off rate, that $15 increases to about $67. (The charge-off rate is the percentage loss resulting from uncollected defaulted debt which is actually experienced.) A securitizing lender with a 50-basis-point annual charge-off rate can increase the $15 to $134. It is a function not only of whether the bank securitizes but also of the expected loss it can show that the structures can be built around. This results in lower overall marketing costs.

Finally, the securitization process provides some external scrutiny and management information that can help make credit enhancers and investors more comfortable with a given portfolio. This is the type of information that senior bank management should have known long before, but never managed to ask.

Question and Answer Session

Question: How can an investor evaluate the quality of loan monitoring done before buying an asset-backed security?

Ocampo: The track record is important. First, look at the kind of asset being pooled. Some of these assets are very difficult to monitor because not enough is known about them. The originator needs an early warning sign that credit is going to be a problem. In the case of trade receivables, a skillful lender has a leading indicator of problems. If a company gets into trouble, it is going to sell less, and its customers will pay late. That shows up immediately in its receivables record. The first question to ask as an investor is, "Can I logically see how I would monitor a portfolio? Do I have a competitive edge in terms of some information value that a nonlender does not have?" Second, look at the company's track record over time.

Make sure the offering does not have a long history of losses relative to some proxy.

Question: What type of asset will be securitized next?

Ocampo: Certain commercial borrowings from non-rated companies—those backed by accounts receivable pools—represent a likely category of expansion.

Question: You illustrated the benefits of removing assets from banks' balance sheets. What are the negative consequences of securitization on the value of banks?

Ocampo: If the transaction is not well structured or properly priced, a securitized deal might cost a bank too much in the way of spread income and leave the bank with an excessive retained-risk position.

Understanding Securitization in Analyzing Common Stock Investments, Part I

William J. Welsh
Vice President, Equity Research
J.P. Morgan Investment Management, Inc.

Do not ever throw a surprise party for a bank analyst. When the guests yell "Surprise!" the analyst is likely to dive into the punch bowl. Bank analysts are nervous, even jumpy, about surprises. I see three reasons for this. First, banks have an inherent bias toward negative surprises. Nobody ever pays back more principal than they borrow, but many pay less. Second, more and more I read that investing in a bank holding company is identical to investing in a blind pool of bad loans, and that the analyst's efforts are futile. Furthermore, bank analysts have not been very popular for the past 15 months. No wonder bank analysts hate surprises.

Unfortunately, this description of banks is not entirely off the mark. Banks operate with very high financial leverage, and bank equity investors are like the credit enhancers of a securitized pool of assets. They incur the first loss. The asset pool is at once more diversified and more complex. Yet, the level of disclosure to bank equity investors is substantially less than the due diligence information available to the credit enhancers. Analysts see only the external books.

In this presentation, I will review the factors that an analyst should understand about securitization and the value of bank stocks. I will begin with an examination of the micro impacts of securitization on banks, followed by a review of the longer-term strategic effects.

Impact of Securitization on Banks

Securitization is changing the way people analyze banks. Both analysts and management must adapt to the changes.

Analysts and investors should view the securitization of bank assets as both a benefit and a threat. At the micro level, securitization is a complication, a tool, and a risk. It is a complication because it changes a bank's sources of income and expenses. For example, by looking at the financial statements of Citicorp, an analyst might conclude that credit card assets have not grown for the past two years. In reality, they have grown steadily, and the income from the securitized card assets is largely retained by Citicorp, but the components of that income on Citicorp's financial statements has changed. The credit losses are reduced. Spread income is not reported as net interest income. Instead, the excess spread income, net of credit losses, appears as other noninterest income on the income statement. As a result, a line-by-line analysis of Citicorp's financial statements would lead an analyst to conclude that Citicorp's margin is weak, and that credit quality and other income is abnormally strong—but these conclusions are not correct. To understand what is really going on, analysts must incorporate the effects of securitization.

More than simply affecting the traditional financial reporting, securitization of bank assets has rendered obsolete the analysts' traditional focus on asset size, growth, and performance. FDIC statistics on bank loans, particularly in the mortgage and installment categories, can no longer be relied upon to reflect demand in the economy or the competitive performance of banks versus other credit suppliers. New measures and new insights are required of analysts and investors.

In spite of all the problems securitization poses for the traditional bank analyst and investor, securitization has proven to be a very powerful tool for bank management. Bank managements now have more options to manage their balance sheets, conserve capital, alter interest rate risk, build liquidity, and lower funding costs. This is especially important in times when bank regulators have increased the pressure on banks to build capital to protect investors and the deposit insurance funds against bank risks. In the past, when a bank fell below minimum capital requirements, management only had four options for remedying the situation: raise capital, reduce dividends, sell entire businesses, or shrink assets. In the current hostile environment for bank investing, no banker wants to issue new equity, and dividend cuts are pure pain. As for selling businesses, although some businesses are expendable, those that bring the best prices are usually the ones that management would least like to sell. The final choice, shrinking businesses, is counter to everyone's basic desire to grow—it is horrible for morale, focuses more management attention on internal turf wars and expense cutting, and detracts from keeping customers satisfied. Compared to these choices, securitization is a "no brainer." The bank does not have to give up its franchise, it retains most of the income from the assets sold, and the lower asset base reduces the need for outside capital.

The situation in the fourth quarter of 1987 illustrates my point. After the stock market crashed, people were concerned about a recession. Assuming a near-term recession scenario with a negative outcome for developing-country loans, I calculated that BankAmerica, which was then selling for $6 a share, might have to issue 1 billion shares at $3 per share to restore its capital base. In other words, meltdown. One of the ways BankAmerica avoided that scenario was to securitize and sell big chunks of its consumer mortgage and installment loan portfolios. Instead of the meltdown scenario, it was able to shrink its need for capital and ultimately issued only 70 million shares at prices averaging nearly $20 a share.

Securitization is also a powerful tool to help banks balance interest rate risk. At the simplest level, banks can continue to offer the 30-year fixed-rate mortgages still preferred by many consumers—without having to find matching funds—by securitizing and selling the assets. More complex structured products like collateralized mortgage obligations (CMOs) and their residuals have created new and unique instruments with sufficient volume and liquidity to enable banks to fine-tune duration matching and manage interest rate risk. Although this has never been as large an issue for banks as for thrifts, it still has improved banks' flexibility.

Asset securitization has greatly enhanced liquidity—or what bank analysts call "the L-word." It used to be that if a bank was called upon to publicly defend its liquidity, it was too late. The events of the past 18 months have proven the importance of liquidity. Several defaults and scares in the investment-grade commercial paper market have made investors very jittery. At the same time, rising fears about bank asset quality and a flood of rating downgrades have combined to make the commercial paper market quite hostile to the banks. Securitization in this time period

has been invaluable in banks' efforts to minimize their dependence on commercial paper funding. Because of the environment of fear, securitizing assets provides funds at lower costs than unsecured bank holding company obligations.

Risks Associated with Securitization

For analysts and investors in bank holding company securities, securitization poses several risks. The largest risk is broadly defined as "rebound risk," the potential loss associated with any residual credit risk exposure to the assets sold by the banks. To determine the magnitude of this risk, analysts routinely examine loan-loss reserve ratios as a percentage of loans or as a percentage of problem loans, and compare banks' relative positions based on these measures and their history. These measures are not meaningful if a bank has a *de facto* exposure to loss for a loan that is no longer on the balance sheet. This *de facto* exposure could take many forms. It could be a cap on loss for the investors in the securitized assets, or a guarantee of repurchase with a price limit. Even when these are carefully structured to meet all the regulatory requirements for removal from the balance sheet, however, there is a vague concern that there is some circumstance under which the bank will have to cover a loss on an asset it did not even know existed.

Another concern is residual credit risk that may not even be reflected as credit losses. In credit card securitization, within certain limits, increases in credit losses on the pool of card loans could reduce the other income by squeezing the excess spread on the loans. Analysts are accustomed to credit losses being cyclical, but they depend on noninterest income to be more stable. This could be a nasty surprise when credit losses rise in a recession, because the bank must absorb a loss of income on more assets than appear on the balance sheet. The result is, if the analyst has not applied as much capital as if the asset were still on the balance sheet, the return on capital will be more volatile than forecast.

There is also a risk of higher loss ratios from negative selection from multi-tiered structured transactions. For example, when bank investors are nervous about the bank's exposures to highly leveraged companies created through LBOs, leveraged acquisitions, and recapitalizations, a bank could reduce its apparent exposure by pooling its exposure to several borrowers into a trust and selling different tranches against the pool. If the bank retains only the longest term or most subordinated tier, its aggregate exposure would be reduced, but its overall risk may be unaltered. In such a case historical loss ratios would no longer apply.

In addition to rebound risk, residual risk, and negative selection, there is novelty or complexity risk. Many of these securities and markets have not been through a full cycle of economic extremes. Therefore, analysts should ask a lot of questions to determine the risk. For example, if interest rates soar or plummet, how will CMO residuals perform? Will they remain liquid or simply freeze up like parts of the junk bond market or the perpetual floating-rate note market? Are we playing musical chairs with these securities? What if unemployment goes back above 10 percent? Are the credit enhancers and loan servicers really prepared for that sort of cyclical rise in credit losses and collection expenses? Suppose they choose not to be involved, or raise the required yield, simply closing the benefits of securitization? If credit losses rise too far, will a bank have to make the investors whole to preserve its reputation, even though it may bear no legally enforceable risk? Do all of the participants fully understand the complexities and the ranges of possible outcomes for these securities? Are they all acting rationally, or is someone making stupid mistakes—taking risks they are not being paid for? These are the kinds of questions that make bank analysts and investors wake up screaming in the night.

The Future Impact of Securitization on Banks

Securitization will affect both the structure and profitability of banking over the next decade or two. The impact of securitization on single-family mortgages is an indication of what will happen in the future. Securitization commoditized the mortgage market, resulting in lower mortgage costs and lower profitability of holding and funding mortgages on bank and thrift balance sheets. The single-family mortgage is a relatively simple financial contract. The home is a single physical asset, the value of which is readily appraisable. The individual borrower has income that is reasonably predictable, assuming they remain employed, and the ratios of loan-to-value and payments-to-income are easily calculated, with minimal uncertainty. Indeed, the risks are actuarially diversifiable, making portfolio performance even more predictable.

Automobile loans and credit card loans have similar characteristics. The combination of securitization and cut-rate financing offered by the automobile finance companies has already eroded returns in the automobile lending market.

The rapid growth of credit card securitization has not yet led to the erosion of the profitability of that business for the issuing banks. Banks are concerned, however, about lower profitability in this area because a number of them depend on the profits of their credit card business to help them earn their way out of their current problems—problems of asset quality and the slowdown of the big-ticket corporate financing business. Credit card lending remains the single highest return-on-asset business in the banking industry.

Although some erosion of return is inevitable, there are several reasons why credit card securitization may continue to expand. First, there are large barriers to entry, and high costs to developing the highly profitable mature accounts. The credit loss experience on newly originated cards is typically three to five times worse than on mature accounts. The only way to avoid this higher credit cost on new accounts is to spend more on screening new applicants and rejecting a higher percentage of the applicants. If a bank decided to cut interest rates during the acquisition and growth phase, entry costs would be increased still higher. It is worth noting that the three largest entries to credit card lending—American Express Optima, Sears Discover, and AT&T Universal—all charge relatively high interest rates for borrowing.

Second, once a bank has achieved a mature, profitable card base, there is no incentive to cut interest rates, which continue to drive the profitability of the business. Consumers have not proven to be sensitive to 2 or 3 percentage point differences in the finance rates. A large card issuer, with a mature card base, would not see sufficient increases in market share from cutting the rates to offset the decline in profitability on their existing card base.

Third, there are limits to how far annual fee reductions and promotional rebates like mileage credits can go to erode profitability. Statistically, about one-third of all credit card holders never borrow against their cards. If fees are eliminated and promotions increased, banks lose money on these nonborrowing customers. These customers are, in essence, loss leaders that show up when a bank is soliciting new customers, and achieves a mix of nonborrowers and the very profitable borrowing customers. Bank card issuers are reluctant to lose too much on the nonborrowing customers, or to be the bank that attracts a higher proportion of nonborrowers.

Commercial loans are another candidate for securitization. The middle-market lending business is the staple of business for so many regional banks. Reduced profitability because of securitization is a concern, but I do not think it will happen. This gets to the fundamental nature of the business of lending money. Lending is a pure value-of-information business. How much information is needed to assure the lender or security investor that they can gauge the risk of loss with enough certainty to enable them to price the credit to reach an acceptable overall rate of profitability? What does it cost to gather, analyze, and disseminate that information in relation to the volume of credit outstanding? For large corporate credits, it costs a great deal to gather and analyze the information, but that cost is spread over a large volume of credit outstanding. For consumer loans and mortgages, at the micro level the information is very simple, and the uncertainty less worrisome; the ability to diversify over large numbers of loans makes the predictability quite satisfactory. But for middle market commercial loans to companies with sales from $5 million to $200 million, the necessary information at the micro level is more complex. The range of potential outcomes for income and cash flow is wider, and the factors that determine those cash flows are more varied. Major debt-raising agencies do not rate these credits because it is too expensive relative to their size.

Large corporations, like Phillip Morris or General Motors, maintain relationships with hundreds of banks. Middle-market companies may deal with only one bank, or perhaps several banks, because there is not enough potential business to justify more institutions devoting the time and expense to gather and monitor the information they would need to compete on extending credit at acceptable rates.

Can the specific risks associated with middle-market commercial loans be diversified? In theory, yes, but this presumes that the sellers of the loans continue to do their homework with the same diligence as when they retained the loan. If the credit enhancer does not do the homework, they may accept more risk than they are being compensated for. If they misprice the risk when the economy is strong, they will get burned on the down cycle; the next time they will demand higher compensation, and securitization will lose popularity. So securitized middle-market loans would not likely be as cheap a source of funding as credit card receivables are today.

Middle-market lending in this country is a very hands-on business. It can be described as driving around in a car that is not very flashy, knocking on sheet metal doors somewhere near a railroad track or dock, in a neighborhood that has very few trendy restaurants. Middle-market lenders are lenders, advisors, and disciplinarians for many of these small businesses. They monitor and keep track of the credit very tightly. Human nature says they would not do so if they were no longer at risk for the assets. Therefore, the moral hazard risk will make it more difficult to securitize these loans over the long term.

Conclusion

Securitization complicates bank analysis and poses certain risks, but provides some excellent tools for managing capital, interest rate risk, funding costs, and liquidity. Despite the discomfort they create for analysts and investors in banks, properly managed securitization programs are a fundamental net positive for bank management in the near and intermediate term.

When analyzing the impact of securitization of assets on the banking industry, there are very visible benefits in capital and balance sheet management. These are achieved with controllable, but not inconsequential, risks. Although securitization may put some pressure on bank profit margins, it is unlikely to destroy the profitability of the more attractive franchises that remain for banks today.

Understanding Securitization in Analyzing Common Stock Investments, Part II

Allan G. Bortel, CFA
Vice President, Corporate Finance
Sutro & Co. Incorporated

When it comes to profitability, the financial services industry has few places left to hide. Improved technology has resulted in overcapacity and reduced profit margins. Securitization, a major technological innovation, has contributed to these developments by homogenizing the U.S. mortgage market. Originators, such as savings and loans (S&Ls), will have to become much more efficient to survive. Other financial services providers are not far behind the S&Ls as victims of technology.

Banks and the S&Ls are showing that they are not immune to the narrowing of spreads throughout the entire financial services industry. The spread squeeze in products beyond mortgages is a strong argument for greater cost efficiency. As a long-time analyst of S&Ls and to some extent of banks, I first look at an entity's capital adequacy and then at its efficiency and attention to cost reduction.

Investment portfolio managers are probably the most immune to technological change. Portfolio management is one field in the whole financial services spectrum that has preserved its margins, and unlike depository institutions, it is a more clear-cut business for the 1990s. Many banks and S&Ls are frightened by securitization, but they have no choice but to accept it. Portfolio managers, as well as consumers, have been well served by securitization.

The thrift industry encompasses two basic types of lenders—portfolio lenders and mortgage bankers. The portfolio lenders keep their loans and earn a spread. Mortgage bankers sell their loans, nowadays usually securitized. Portfolio lenders were among the first buyers of mortgage-backed securities in the early 1970s. At that time, the spread over the thrift cost of funds was still fairly attractive. They cannot be counted on to invest in mortgage-backed securities much longer, however, even though new risk-based capital rules promote investment in securitized mortgages as opposed to conventional home loans, commercial loans, and construction loans. Their capital

and funding costs are too high to justify holding only securitized mortgages.

Risk-Based Capital Requirements

Figure 1 shows risk-weighted baskets for the various assets that thrifts may hold. To the left, at zero weighting, are Ginnie Mae securities and cash. The 20 percent basket contains Federal Home Loan Bank stock and mortgage-backed securities of the Federal National Mortgage Association (Fannie Mae) and Federal Home Loan Mortgage Corporation (Freddie Mac).

The next basket, with a 50 percent risk weighting, includes one- to four-family home loans not enhanced by Fannie Mae and Freddie Mac guarantees. Securitization has brought mortgage rates down, helping the consumer but not the taxpayer. Under the new risk-based capital rules, the risk is placed on the taxpayer in a different way—an implied guarantee that Fannie Mae and Freddie Mac are backed by the taxpayer, who is now the lender of last resort. For a guarantee fee paid to these agencies, the portfolio lender has reduced credit risk in its portfolio and complied with the new risk-based capital rules—shifting the risk to the agencies.

Not all types of assets are shown in Figure 1, and various conditions apply. Private-issue, mortgage-backed securities, for example, must be "high-quality" one- to four-family residential mortgage loans and are limited to those prudently underwritten, performing not more than 90 days past due with a documented loan-to-value ratio not exceeding 80 percent at origination, unless insured to at least 80 percent by private mortgage insurance issued by a Freddie Mac- or Fannie Mae-approved insurer. Multifamily residential mortgages are limited to existing 5- to 36-unit properties with an initial loan-to-value ratio not exceeding 80 percent and having an average annual occupancy of 80 percent or more of total units for at least one year.

Figure 1. Risk-Weighted Assets for Savings Associations (FIRREA Basket Ratios)

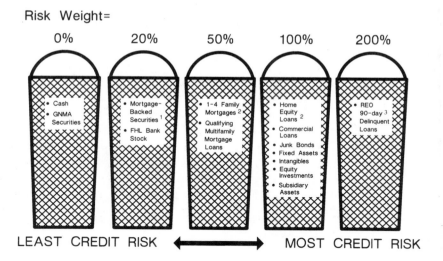

Risk Weight=

| 0% | 20% | 50% | 100% | 200% |

- Cash
- GNMA Securities

- Mortgage-Backed Securities [1]
- FHL Bank Stock

- 1-4 Family Mortgages [2]
- Qualifying Multifamily Mortgage Loans

- Home Equity Loans [2]
- Commercial Loans
- Junk Bonds
- Fixed Assets
- Intangibles
- Equity Investments
- Subsidiary Assets

- REO
- 90-day [3] Delinquent Loans

LEAST CREDIT RISK ⟷ MOST CREDIT RISK

[1] Mortgage-backed securities with residual or stripped features go into the 100 percent basket.

[2] Office of Thrift Supervision may issue a "marginal" capital rule applicable to these assets that bases the relevant risk basket on the loan-to-value ratio. Loans with low loan-to-value ratios will go into a low-percentage basket; those with higher ratios into higher percentage baskets.

[3] Ninety-day delinquent one- to four-family mortgages go into the 100 percent basket.

Source: Pulles, Gregory J. 1990. *A Director's Guide to the New Capital Rules.* Minneapolis: Merrill Corporation (January).

Generally, when assets flunk the test for one level, they move to the next highest risk basket.

The Financial Institutions Reform, Recovery and Enforcement Act of 1989 (FIRREA) pinpointed risks to savings institutions and encouraged them to pay the Fannie Mae and Freddie Mac guarantee fee. These agencies are running a booming business. Fannie Mae will have nearly $300 billion of mortgage securities guaranteed by the end of this year, and the business did not start up until the end of 1982. About 15 percent of all one- to four-unit residential loans are securitized by Fannie Mae. A very cynical attitude toward securitization and risk-based capital rules is that Fannie Mae and Freddie Mac stockholders have been helped, while the S&L portfolio lenders take most of the risks. The S&Ls take in the money, lend it, and make the spread, but their expenses are so high that they do not make much money. The best operators in the portfolio lending business, a couple of public companies on the West Coast, make a 17 to 18 percent return on equity because they have concentrated on cost control—not a very impressive return given the cyclical risks.

Mortgage Banking

The mortgage banking business tends to be run by only a few people with that type of experience. Their business is originating, selling, and servicing mortgages. Selling servicing rights was the key to profitability for them, but now servicing rights are going at about half the price of a year ago because (1) the Federal Deposit Insurance Corporation (FDIC) has proposed capping the purchase of mortgage servicing rights, and (2) the Resolution Trust Corporation (RTC) has some $150 billion of servicing rights for sale.

Because servicing is merely a strip of revenue from the mortgage lending process, the mortgage lending game is not as attractive as it used to be. These days, a mortgage banking-oriented S&L has to do two or three times more volume than previously in order to create servicing. Furthermore, the new risk-based rules will make S&Ls more cautious about taking risks on their mortgage pipelines.

The Market for Mortgage-Backed Securities

Various thrift organizations deal in mortgage-backed securities. Of the top 25 thrift stocks listed by *American Banker*, only two large ones, H. F. Ahmanson and Great Western Financial, create mortgage-backed securities. Both have tried to create a market for an adjustable-rate mortgage-backed security, but they have been unsuccessful, largely because Fannie Mae and Freddie Mac keep alive the fixed-rate mortgage loan to compete with them.

A number of S&Ls trade mortgage-backed securities actively, and the empirical evidence indicates that active traders of mortgage-backed securities sell their winners and keep their losers. In the end, RTC sees the evidence of this as it sifts through the ashes of some of the balance sheets of thrifts.

The best-run thrifts probably will be able to realize 15 to 20 percent returns on equity, but not through mortgage-backed securities. The attitude at Golden West (strictly a portfolio lender) is, "If we securitize, why should we pay Fannie Mae or Freddie Mac 15 or 20 basis points?" Some large S&Ls have engineered deals with Fannie Mae and Freddie Mac to get lower than average guarantee fees, illustrating the buying power of large organizations.

Fannie Mae and Freddie Mac

Fannie Mae and Freddie Mac are a boon to consumers of residential mortgage credit. Through the work of these organizations, loan discount points have been reduced, bond market pricing has improved, and the availability of mortgage funds has increased. Unfortunately, however, these agencies may also exacerbate the S&L profit crisis by lowering mortgage rates and squeezing S&L margins.

Fannie Mae and Freddie Mac often publicize their transactions by advertising what they are doing for securitization and homeowners. In part, this advertising is in response to congressional pressure to enhance the capital base of the two agencies. S&L industry executives are frustrated that the agencies do not have to abide by the same capital guidelines that they do. The loans Fannie Mae owns are no different than the residential loans against which S&Ls must retain much larger amounts of capital.

If Congress requires Fannie Mae and Freddie Mac to have greater capital, the agencies may have to raise the price of their services, if they can. The new head of Fannie Mae has his job cut out for him in dealing with the Treasury Department and the administration on that point. Because of revenue shortfalls, Congress probably will not come to the aid of Fannie Mae as it has in the past. In fact, some members of Congress are starting to relate the securitization pressure on Fannie Mae and Freddie Mac to the cost of the S&L bailout. The agencies realize that they are not immune to requirements to beef up their own capital.

The enhancement of the quality of the security and of credit are certainly on the minds of people at the Treasury because of the S&L bailout. They see Fannie Mae and Freddie Mac as friends of S&Ls in supplying them with liquidity and in creating the ability to repossess loans; they also see them as foes that are narrowing spreads and squeezing the industry. This is part of the whole picture in financial services, which as an industry is feeling the squeeze. The interplay of Congress; the Treasury; Fannie Mae; Freddie Mac; and investment portfolio, bank, and S&L players in the market for securities is critical and a scene the investor should not ignore.

Conclusion

Securitization has not been kind to the thrift industry. Securitization of mortgage-backed securities has resulted in narrower profit margins and severe distress for most thrifts. The growing spread squeeze in products beyond mortgages makes an even stronger argument for greater cost efficiency for financial institutions and concern by regulators.

Question and Answer Session

Question: From a risk-based capital perspective, should purchased servicing rights be viewed differently than excess servicing rights?

Bortel: "Purchased" servicing rights are assets for which someone else has created the stream of income by originating a mortgage loan and has sold the rights to service it. "Excess" servicing rights are the so-called assets arising from future streams of income related to servicing a loan beyond the normal cost associated with the servicing activity. The lender develops this income stream when it originates and sells a loan. It is basically the accounting recognition of creating an asset, although cash has not yet been received for the future servicing.

Excess servicing rights caused some famous accounting problems a few years ago. One company, City Federal (New Jersey), had a tremendous amount of excess servicing on its books, and those loans paid off much earlier than had been estimated when the servicing was created. Of course, the S&L had to write that asset way down. In reality, the excess servicing was not a good asset, even though it had been recognized as future income. City Federal has since been taken over by the RTC.

Purchased, or outstanding, servicing usually has a track record of some sort. In fact, if you buy seasoned servicing, you can hedge it better than you can your own servicing. Hedge contracts are now available from some of the major securities dealers.

Servicing is an intriguing part of the mortgage business. The industry is currently evolving as efficient subservicers grow and very large blocks of servicing contracts trade between buyers and sellers. The government does not want the banks and savings and loans to acquire servicing because it believes servicing is a volatile asset without any good way of hedging against the risks of early payoff of an underlying loan. One would think that guidelines could be established as to what is risky and what is not risky in purchasing servicing rights. This is an untracked, uncharted field that regulators, given all of the other problems, do not want to tackle. Someone should tackle it, however, because of the huge drop in servicing values that has occurred in the past year in response to uncertainty about proposed capital rules and about the RTC's selling program.

Question: What do you think is going to happen to the U.S. banking market? Will it be able to compete with the financially strong international institutions?

Welsh: Yes, I think so. The Japanese banks are not as strong financially as they once were. They have recently been downgraded, or are in the process of being downgraded, and probably will continue to be as a result of their exposures to real estate and highly leveraged transaction lending. The European banks, particularly the German and Swiss banks, are better capitalized than the U.S. banks.

Over time, the industry will see more consolidation and a lot more intramarket mergers, perhaps even the combination of some of the large New York banks. I doubt this will happen, however, until we are beyond the current concern about asset quality, unless deals can be done on a firendly basis. No one has the financial strength to be the acquirer right now, and nobody wants to be the acquiree. If the deal is unfriendly, then the acquirer cannot look at the books. If that is the case, concern about the unknown asset-quality problems the acquirer may be buying will make its stock price drop like a stone on the day it tries to make an acquisition. So, we will see a hiatus in merger activity for a couple of years and then a revival, with particular emphasis on the intramarket deals, which have been proven to be beneficial, as demonstrated by the merger of Wells Fargo and Crocker.

Question: What is the probability of a breakthrough next year on allowing the corporate sector to inject capital into the banking sector, obviously in return for control of certain ownership aspects?

Welsh: That is possible, but probably only in a true crisis. The dismantling of Glass-Steagall and the separation of banking from the commercial markets had been occurring slowly, primarily driven by the courts and the regulators. Congress has done very little to relax restrictions on banking. Congressmen never want to settle, because once they do, someone will be upset and stop donating money to their campaigns. As long as they keep the ball in the air, the insurance industry, the banks, the S&Ls, and the brokers continue to contribute. The regulars are pushing this and the courts are defending it, but the idea of industrial companies buying banks is a large enough leap that it probably cannot be done without congressional action, except in a crisis.

Question: Do you think banks will compete for credit

card business by offering multilevel interest rates?

Welsh: You have already seen some tiering like that. Banks have traditionally found that their branch-customer cardholders have much lower loss ratios than the cardholders they got through direct-mail marketing. So you see lower rates for multiple accounts. Some banks charge lower financing rates for larger balances and for customers with higher incomes. This will not happen much, however, because people are willing to pay the higher rates; they view the product as a convenience. For a large card issuer, reducing the rate enough to get people to switch to your bank card will cost so much in lost income that it is not cost effective. Many efforts have been made to impose usury ceilings on credit card rates, but they always die for lack of support.

Question: Please comment on General Electric's future as a financial services company and the recent story on it in *Barron's*.

Bortel: I have not read that story. Its thesis is probably that GE is the next big accident waiting to happen in financial services. I am in the other camp. I believe that companies like GE have the future to themselves in terms of technology. They do not have the bricks and mortar and redundant facilities of the thrifts and commercial banks. Also, the banks and thrifts are under stress from their problem real estate loans and are having to fall back on low-profit businesses. Now we are talking about lower profit margins on credit cards because of securitization. We are facing a new situation when companies like Westinghouse and GE are the future deliverers of financial services. Merrill Lynch and Shearson, with their central asset accounts, made a good stab at it, and so did First Boston by delivering mortgage credit via computer. This is how those trends start. Someone tries it, fails, and then someone else tries it again and finally gets it through.

Inevitably, computer technology will overwhelm the financial services industry. Securitization came about because of advances in technology. Following the S&Ls and banks is a tough job, and the environment is changing radically. The days of branch banks and Regulation Q are over, yet many of the banks and S&Ls have not modified their thinking.

The head of the New York Stock Exchange came back from Russia and said something like, "Those people might never have a stock exchange, or it will be a long time before they can create one." That is malarkey. Why do they need people running around on a floor? We could sell them all the computer hardware and software they need to create active financial markets. The buyers and sellers do not have to be matched up by telephone or by face-to-face market dealings; they could leapfrog into the securitized, computerized era that we have helped to develop.

Question: Please comment on the S&L situation.

Bortel: The lobbyists are being overwhelmed by the S&L depositor bailout. Members of Congress go home, hear the anger of their constituents, and come back and turn a deaf ear to bank and S&L lobbyists. Congress is going to examine the whole deposit insurance question, and we are in for some major changes. Financial services changes have not come rapidly through regulation, but the $500 billion S&L depositor bailout will force Congress to take a swat at major changes in regulations, which will probably not benefit most banks and S&Ls.

Question: What banks and thrifts do you think we should buy today, if any?

Welsh: The investment markets are so spooked by the problem of credit quality that they are discounting a major depression in the economy for bank stocks, but that outcome has not yet been reflected in the rest of the market. If we have a really stiff, deep, long recession, you probably should not own bank stock. If somehow the economy avoids disaster, then you can probably throw darts at the list, because the financial institutions have all been taken down with the assumption of severe credit problems. A number of very well-capitalized companies have limited exposure to the riskiest segments of the economy, particularly real estate and the highly leveraged transaction loans, and these are clearly going to survive. The day will come when people will stop focusing on how far down we can go and start thinking about what the upside will be when we get past this recession. That could be the day the Fed eases aggressively. Some other event could be what changes the psychology, but a vast majority of companies are going to survive this current bout with credit problems.

The Effects of Securitization on Bank Regulation in the 1990s

Owen Carney
Director, Investment Securities Division
Office of the Comptroller of the Currency

From a regulator's perspective, regulation in the 1990s is not going to be any easier than it was in the 1980s. Regulators have two choices: (1) to be reactive and wait for things to happen, or (2) to be proactive and try to prevent problems. I believe that the best form of regulation is the preventive style, in which the regulator—in our case the examiner, who is the primary line of regulation—focuses on the causes of potential problems, rather than waiting for problems to emerge and devoting full energies to discovering specific details. Discovering existing problems is not hard. Examiners can become pretty accurate at shooting wounded people. Prevention by focusing on the causes of potential problems is far more difficult.

Securitization represents a significant change for the commercial banking industry. In fact, it is probably the most fundamental change in the past 50 years, and the long-range effect of securitization has yet to be seen.

In dealing with a new activity, most regulators try to strike a balance. We are loathe to smother a new banking activity with regulatory burdens. On the other hand, changes in the banking system all too often have not received the appropriate amount of regulatory attention because the significance of the change is not recognized early enough—sometimes because the changes themselves are not fully understood, and sometimes because the regulators simply have their hands full with other problems.

Securitization is different from other innovations. Unlike most "new" innovations, when you break securitization down into its component pieces, it involves traditional banking activities—loan originations, servicing, credit enhancement or guarantees, underwriting, distribution, syndications, banks functioning as corporate trustees, and banks functioning as investors. None of these functions is new to the banking system. The regulators are accustomed to dealing with each of these components. What they have not dealt with in the past is the process on a combined basis.

When securitization first became apparent to us,

the Comptroller staff had a different name for it: deposit substitute programs. I believe this is still the prevailing attitude. From the issuer's perspective, securitization is a different way of obtaining funds for traditional banking activities. As the activities funded in this manner became a separate line of business, the line of business itself introduced different types of regulatory concerns. The risks and benefits associated with the traditional banking activities are well known to the regulators. Now, we have had enough experience with some incipient problems in securitization to convince us that we need to devote a considerable amount of resources to examination of the securitization functions in banks.

The focus of our securitization examination effort has been on how well bankers self-regulate the activity of originating for resale, including controls and accounting practices. The results of the examinations have been mixed. Some banks accomplish different parts of this process very well, but almost nobody does everything very well. There is always some glitch, which is to be expected with any new product line.

We are gratified to see that the securitization process in most banks is in the hands of the traditional credit divisions rather than the investment banking divisions. The regulators' worst fear about securitization is that it will be dominated by the investment banking culture. Our view is that the commercial banking division can add stability to the process of securitization and will devote the types of resources necessary to appropriate standards of credit underwriting, credit administration, and credit service. Without these standards, the entire process of securitization is at risk. We do not want people who have an instant-gratification mentality to take control of securitization and simply produce credits for the sake of producing volume.

In addition to our examination focus, we are attempting to develop supervisory policy standards that will focus on a more thoughtful overall regulatory approach to securitization.

The Focus of Regulatory Efforts

The overall regulatory approach of the Comptroller's office to securitization is focused on four areas: (1) accounting; (2) risk-based capital; (3) new powers for banks, and how we as an agency might address the need for new powers in banks in conjunction with their securitization activities; and (4) investment limitations—that is, limitations on banks acting as investors. We are reviewing all of these in an environment that is rapidly changing—the level of credit risk in the environment is changing, and securitization is introducing dramatic changes into relationship banking. At the same time, we are actively considering competitive factors.

Accounting

For a number of years, regulators have made an earnest attempt to reconcile and eliminate differences between regulatory accounting principles and generally accepted accounting principles (GAAP). Lately, however, this attitude has changed as we realized that accounting has not kept pace with changes in business practices and new product developments. Also, accountants are under considerable pressure from clients who want results that may not be the most prudent from a regulatory perspective. We have also come to understand that we cannot wait for the sometimes agonizingly slow process of modifying existing accounting standards to deal with new products.

With respect to securitization accounting, we are having a great deal of trouble accepting GAAP treatment of sales versus borrowing. We find FAS 77, which is the governing standard in this area, to be an easily manipulated accounting standard. FAS 77 focuses on the retention of benefits, rather than on the retention of risk, as the point of demarcation for determining sale versus financing treatment. As regulators, we are very concerned with the existence of risk. We assume that benefits will work their way out through the system.

We have also had a lot of problems with the timing of recognition of income. Securitization involves a change for banks from a spread-management form of income recognition to a fee-based system of income recognition. The most aggressive styles of accounting would permit virtually instant recognition of the current value of future income, even though the income has not been received and investors might still have claims against some of that income. As a result, in the course of some of our securitization examinations to date, we have begun to question assumptions having to do with income and expense recognition and the timing of both. This is going to be a critical factor in influencing how people securitize.

If you view securitization as an obvious response to risk-based capital, you can understand why we are so sensitive to sale treatment. Right now, the regulations require capital support for assets that are on the books and for contingent liabilities that are recognizable and measurable. On the other hand, FAS 77 permits assets to be taken off the books when the seller is in a position to estimate their liabilities under whatever recourse positions exist in the sale. The seller then reserves the full amount of those recourse liabilities. Our experience with this kind of assumption-driven accounting has not been good.

The Federal Financial Institution Examination Council (FFIEC) (which is the coordinating umbrella for the Federal Reserve, the Federal Deposit Insurance Corporation, the National Credit Union Administration, the Conference of State Bank Supervisors, and the Office of Thrift Supervision) has issued a proposal for public comment on how a bank's recourse obligations in this area should be regulated. We are seeking input on how to account for securitization and appropriate levels of risk-based capital, with particular emphasis on recourse: how to define recourse, how to report sales with recourse, and appropriate capital to support recourse.

We have received about 150 comment letters to date. They could be categorized as follows: absolutely incomprehensible (only two); those dealing with Veterans Administration (VA) servicing (an unusually strident and impassioned series of letters that spoke to veterans' benefits, housing, and so forth); and extremely lengthy, thoughtful arguments about approaches that regulators should take to securitization and recourse. We are in the process of actively digesting those letters. I am not sure exactly where they are going to take us.

As regulators, we are concerned with several aspects of seller-provided recourse. We are concerned about seller's warranties and representations, particularly when the warranties and representations that are given are not completely within the control of the seller. An example is the uninsured hazard representation—when a seller represents that he will reimburse an investor for any damages suffered from uninsured hazards, such as earthquakes. Another example is the environmental warranty—when a seller represents to a buyer that all the properties involved in a sale are in full compliance with environmental health and safety laws. Generally, these types of hazards and environmental issues are not within the control of the seller. To the extent that guarantees are on items under the control of the seller, we will accept them.

Limited recourse arrangements are another area of concern, and one on which we have received a number of comments. A number of these people want us to give special treatment to cases in which the seller agrees to absorb (guarantee) a limited amount of losses, for example 5 to 7 percent of exposure. It would certainly be in the regulators' interest to encourage people to take limited exposures rather than full exposures.

Another area that received a lot of comment was senior/subordinated structures and what to do with subordinated structures retained by sellers. From a regulatory perspective, we view the retention of the subordinated piece by the seller as recourse. The problem becomes a great deal more complicated when you have multiple classes of subordinated credits. Making the call is easy for a simple two-class senior/subordinated structure, but for five classes, it gets a lot more complicated. We are still trying to determine how to deal with the multiclass subordinated structures.

Risk-Based Capital

The issue of determining appropriate capital levels is controversial. One problem that has become very apparent in securitization is the effect of regulation on competition and the burden that regulations place on banks. We are considering the effects of competition and the inequalities that result from regulatory burdens in the way we assess risk-based capital. The arguments concerning unequal competition can only go so far, however. A bank may not be able to compete on an equal footing with retailers, automobile manufacturers, communications conglomerates, or with anything else that is not a bank, but banks are going to be regulated as banks.

At this time, my group will not focus on interest rate risk for purposes of risk-based capital in connection with securitization. Various international committees are working on our approach to interest rate risk for purposes of capital, so we will defer decisions on these matters for now.

One of the recourse issues that most people have not focused on, but which is something that may affect both investors and issuers, is the concept of double count. If we, as regulators, assess 100 percent risk-weighting against a seller who provides recourse, what do we assess the bank that is an investor? The seller's assessment provides a single risk that is embodied in a securitized pool of assets. Should investors in that pool receive a free capital ride, or should they be assessed at another level of capital? That is, should we require more capital for that $1 of risk throughout the system than we would for assets that are retained on a bank's books? If the answer is yes, clearly some elements of unfairness are present.

To the extent that we try to avoid double count-

ing, we also provide a very strong incentive for banks to invest in assets that someone else originates and securitizes. Why should a community bank pay a 100 percent risk-weighting on loans that it makes within its own community if it could get a zero percent risk-weighting on loans that were securitized with recourse by a large regional bank? We have not come to grips with this problem. If we completely avoid the double count, we provide an incentive to internalize the securitization process—for example, banks buying from other banks. If we knowingly tax banks on a double-count basis, we provide an incentive for banks to sell to nonbanks.

Another dimension of the recourse issue that we have not yet been able to deal with is moral recourse. What do we do with banks that have no contractual liability to buy back assets that might go bad but, in practice, choose to buy back assets in order to preserve their reputation and market share or for other reasons? We will probably do what we have done in the past: require more capital, perhaps more than the bank demonstrating a clear pattern of buying back loans is prepared to pay.

The issue of risk-based premium deposit insurance will be important in the 1990s and may provide a strong motivation for expanding securitization. I can easily see a time when the issues of risk premiums on deposit insurance and capital become so significant that banks all over the country might choose to securitize assets. For example, banks in California might offer new accounts two choices: an insured deposit at a given rate, or a piece of a mutual fund composed of loans to small businesses in Silicon Valley that would be uninsured and offered at a higher rate.

New Powers for Banks

As regulators, we have to consider the wisdom of new powers for banks. The growth of securitization is altering the types of activities in which banks are involved. We see a potential for significant expansion in the distribution of securitized bank assets, primarily through public underwritings, private placements, and mutual funds. Private placements would go to the most sophisticated segments of the market, and other pools of securitized assets may be sold to the retail public through mutual funds. The private placement rules have changed recently. I believe the rules will promote banks' use of the private placement vehicle to market their own securitized assets. We have started to see this already, and we expect the pace to continue.

Investment Limitations

We are taking a fairly conservative approach to investment limitations on bank investors in securitized assets. Our current position is that we look to the originator of the credits as the obligor, whether or not the originator of the credit is obligated to make any payments. Much of what is happening in the securitization process, particularly in connection with publicly traded securities, is being driven by the originator—for example, the originator's credit underwriting and collection standards. Investors look at the credit enhancers and the servicers, not at the underlying borrowers individually. A number of people have asked us to base investment limits on something other than the originator of the credits—for example, basing limits on each of the underlying borrowers. That is not acceptable to us. We have also had people ask for separate limitations on each of the trusts that an originator might establish as its issuance vehicle. To date, the answer on that has also been no.

We have been fairly uniform in our decisions, believing that prudent investors should impose their own limitations on their holdings by originator, credit enhancer, servicer, trustee, or packager. Investors should determine how badly they might get hurt from having a concentration and establish their own limitations accordingly. To the extent that banks are not prepared to establish those limits that way, the examiners are. Regulators are enforcing a legal limitation based on originator plus enhancer. They are imposing prudent limitations on trustees, packagers, and servicers.

Changes in the Credit Markets

The credit markets are changing, and the changes will affect banks. For example, the forms of consumer credit have changed greatly. Clearly, there has been a tax-induced shift away from traditional forms of consumer borrowing (credit cards, automobile paper, and so forth) toward home equity loans. I am not sure what this says about consumer credit in the future, but I have some feeling for what it says about borrowers. First, it says that in the future people who take out automobile loans probably do not have equity in their homes or they do not understand the tax code. Will everyone who pays taxes and has sufficient equity in a home choose home equity lines rather than automobile financing? What does this say about the bor-

rowers for automobiles? Does this say they have less of a cushion to fall back on than they once did? I suspect so. I am not sure that the actuarial experience associated with traditional consumer lending is going to be valid through the 1990s. Are we in a new game?

Second, securitization is changing relationships between banks and their customers, particularly the consumer borrowers. Securitization is not something that appeals to or is needed by all banks. To the extent that a bank is placing a premium on relationship banking, securitization is not going to make it any easier. Securitization will certainly depersonalize some aspects of credit underwriting and credit collection, but will it change the way people do business with banks? The loyalties people might have had and the obligations they felt might change along with the relationship. I do not know what effect these factors might have on borrower performance or community service by banks. I do know, however, that the game and the rules are changing.

Conclusion

I spent some time last week at the mortgage bankers' convention in Chicago and listened to a number of banks and insurance companies that wore two hats: securitization hats and investor hats. Their thinking could not have been any more disparate. The investors wanted as much information as they could possibly get, and the securitizers wanted to come out with as general a standard as they could possibly give. We have not seen the reconciliation of the differences yet, and the securitization market is not going to do much beyond securitized consumer credits until we come to some resolution of what information needs to be made available to investors—for example, what it takes to get commercial loans done.

Decisions by regulators will shape the course of securitization throughout the 1990s. We are trying to keep the process as pure as possible. To the extent that a bank sells assets without any recourse, we want to ensure that no recourse exists from that point forward. We also want to ensure that investors are prepared to provide a level of market discipline to the process by making their investment decisions based on the contractual obligations of the seller, the strength of the enhancer, or the underlying credits.

Question and Answer Session

Question: Please discuss the regulatory and investor problems of Federal Housing Administration (FHA) Title 1?

Carney: My biggest concern about FHA Title 1 paper (securitized mobile-home loans with minor FHA support) is that people believe it is government guaranteed. The prospectuses on securitized FHA Title 1 deals clearly state that they are not government guaranteed; they are subsidized by fairly small originator-provided dealer reserves. These reserves start out at about 10 percent, but on average they probably are somewhere in the range of 4 to 5 percent of the originating lender's outstanding loans. That is the only form of guarantee the paper has. Unfortunately, if you read some of the sales literature being put out by brokerage firms, you would think you are buying a government-guaranteed piece of paper.

I am also concerned because I'm not sure that many of the packages out there have provided for a transfer-of-the-payment mechanism. The payments that are made by borrowers, the payments that come from reserve funds, get paid to the originating institution, which in turn commits to pass these payments along. Normally, this would not bother me, but many of the originating institutions are thrifts that are in trouble, and I wonder about a transition. Who gets those payments during the transition period?

Having said that, I think it is probably fine paper. There are a number of bizarre intricacies associated with this. If you understand them and are still willing to do the deal, it is probably okay, but the understanding is a very important part of the limitations embodied in these deals.

Question: Do you think commercial loans will be securitized?

Carney: Yes; it's only a matter of time. But I think for these securities to be successful, there will have to be a significant amount of credit enhancement and a major emphasis on the originating bank's track record. This will be a complicated process.

Question: How big do you think the securitization market will be next year?

Carney: I don't know, but bigger than last year is a safe answer.

Question: If FAS 77 is no good, what guidelines should be used?

Carney: How about the truth? If a seller retains all the normal risks in a securitized credit, it should not get sale treatment for risk-based capital.

The Future of Securitization

Dexter Senft
Managing Director
The First Boston Corporation

The future of securitization is a topic that Yogi Bera would not approve of. Yogi said, "One should never forecast anything, especially the future," but also said, "You can observe a lot just by watching." If one looks at today's securitized markets (mortgages and asset-backed securities) to see how we got here, it is not difficult to make forecasts about the future.

The future of securitization is linked to its history. Therefore, I will begin with a review of the history of securitization. I will look at the *assets* that are likely to be securitized, if they have not been already; the *countries* that are likely to be players—the new markets that will open in the forthcoming months and years; and the *obstacles* that lie between here and there. I will also address the following statements and show you why I think they are *wrong*:

- It would be easy to say that we have only scratched the surface in terms of the assets, and that every asset under the sun will be securitized in the future.
- Technology will be exported from the United States to all worldwide capital markets.

The History of Securitization

The history of securitization is relatively short. Mortgage-backed securities came along in 1970, courtesy of the Government National Mortgage Association (Ginnie Mae); collateralized mortgage obligations (CMOs) began in 1983, but they were nothing new from a securitization standpoint—they were still mortgages, although the structure was different.

The asset-backed securities market started in 1985. In 1985 and 1986, a number of asset-backed securities were issued, all of which had an asset as underlying collateral. The assets included automobile loans, loans on other types of vehicles, and equipment leases. Asset-backed securities were the analogue of mortgage-backed securities until 1987. In other words, when auto loans were converted into asset-backed securities, automobiles were the ultimate collateral, similar to buildings being the ultimate collateral in mortgage-backed securities.

This changed in 1987 with credit card-backed securities, which were securitized by promises to pay, not collateral. The majority of the securities that came after 1987 fall into that category. Other securitized assets included affiliate notes, insurance policy loans, and hospital receivables. In 1989, home equity loans and junk bonds were collateralized. The home-equity loans had collateral, but junk bonds did not, unless they were secured. **Exhibit 1** shows the history of assets securitized.

In terms of asset classes, the future of the asset-backed market is in middle-market commercial and industrial loans as well as less-developed-country (LDC) debt. Both of these are likely to use noncollateralized structures. Securitization may also be used with leveraged buyout (LBO) debts and/or bridge loans, which is a logical evolution of existing CMO structures used in the junk bond market.

Constraints on the Growth of Securitization

The biggest constraint on the growth of securitization has been finding acceptable solutions to the myriad problems arising from peculiarities of assets. Some serious mathematical problems had to be solved before asset securitization became viable. The problems relating to the largest and easiest asset classes have been *solved*, and I use the word quite literally. For example, before the first automobile deal could be done, a mathematician had to prove that there was cash flow sufficiency in auto loans after they were converted from Rule of 78 amortization to a more standard, "economic" amortization schedule. Other asset classes had similar problems that made securitization unfeasible until such problems were solved. This is especially true when looking at the assets in the foreign markets, where they do not always work the same way as in the United States.

The law of diminishing returns is another constraint. The quantity of the asset class must be sufficiently large to make securitizing it worthwhile.

Another constraint is the limited marketability of

Exhibit 1. Securitized Asset Classes

1970:	Mortgages
1985:	Autos
	Boats
	Equipment leases
1986:	RV's
	Light trucks
1987:	Credit cards
	Consumer loans
	Trucks
	Trade receivables
1988:	Affiliate notes
	Insurance policy loans
	Hospital receivables
1989:	Home equity loans
	Time shares
	Junk bonds
1990+:	Middle-market C&I loans
	LDC debt

certain assets. Marketability is the ability to sell an asset quickly at a price. Marketability is often confused with liquidity, which is the ability to sell an asset quickly at the best *available* price. Securities are liquid; washing machines are marketable; some junk bonds and LDC loans are neither. As a rule, asset-backed securities add liquidity, not marketability. You can take assets that are marketable, securitize them, and increase their liquidity. You cannot take unmarketable assets and make them so by putting them into asset-backed securities.

Despite these constraints, I am not forecasting a slow death of the asset-backed securities market. On the contrary, there is strong evidence that the volumes are going to increase as more domestic players get involved. But from a product development standpoint, I see no fundamental innovations in the near term.

New Markets

The five countries that have been the chief issuers of mortgage- or asset-backed securities are the United States, the United Kingdom, Canada, Australia, and France. It is not a coincidence that four out of five are English-speaking countries. It is easier to export American financial technology when you communicate in English.

Several non-English speaking countries are likely to develop mortgage-backed or asset-backed securities markets. These include Japan, Sweden, Germany, and Holland. In Japan I see a large potential for asset-backed securities, probably greater than for mortgage-backed securities. Germany and Holland are both situations in which securitization is possible but not as likely, because of the constraints I shall explain shortly.

Many people are amazed there is not already a mortgage- and asset-backed market in Japan. After all, Japanese investors own large amounts of U.S. mortgage securities, and the Ministry of Finance in Japan recently gave permission to Citicorp to sell its asset-backed securities there. However, these are not examples in which Japanese asset-backed securities are being created or traded, so for my purposes they do not count.

There are basically two constraints to expanding securitization around the globe. First, the country must have a capital market that has some depth and breadth. An asset- or mortgage-backed security cannot be the most complicated thing that market has ever seen. You do not want derivative instruments to be a huge leap from something already going on. In other words, the capital market has to be ready for the technology.

Second, there must be a desire or need to sell assets. That is what created the mortgage and CMO markets in this country: the mortgage market had more supply than demand. Originally, the demand for mortgages came entirely from the bank and thrift industry. Mortgage-backed securities were a way of adding breadth to the market. CMOs broadened the market even further because they brought pension funds into the market.

There is no excess supply of mortgages in Japan. Japanese banks have more than enough money. The spreads they receive make them perfectly happy, and they look at you like you are crazy when you discuss securitizing mortgages. Japan has a capital market that is sophisticated enough, but it does not need to sell the assets. Asset-backed securities (other than mortgages) are a different story, however; they could show up in Japan, but mortgage-backed securities probably will not in the near term. Considering the two constraints together, I see the United Kingdom, Canada, Australia, and France as the most promising markets.

Market Complexity for Asset-Backed Securities

Asset-backed securities are not likely to follow the lead of mortgage-backed securities with respect to complexity. To understand why, let us look at complexity in the mortgage market more closely.

The complexity of the CMO market continues to increase, as it sets new records in terms of volume, breadth, and depth. Breadth may be thought of as the number of tranche types. From 1983 (when the market started) to 1987, the number of tranches per new issue CMO was 4.0; in 1988 it increased to 5.8; in 1989, 9.0; and in 1990, 11.3, and the number is rising. Thus, the growth in tranche types is a recent phenomenon. Some people feel that this growth reflects the fact that the market is supplying value by focusing on specific kinds of risks at the requests of specific investors. Other investors say that the increased complexity is a way to hide risks, and as a result, somebody is getting ripped off. Both explanations are partly true, partly false.

The depth of the market may be viewed in terms of levels of intermediation. **Figure 1** illustrates an actual CMO structure with four different levels of intermediation. Conventional mortgages were bought by the Federal National Mortgage Association (Fannie

but the problems regulators will face will be more complex than mere double counting.[1] Each mortgage in this example could be counted up to four times.

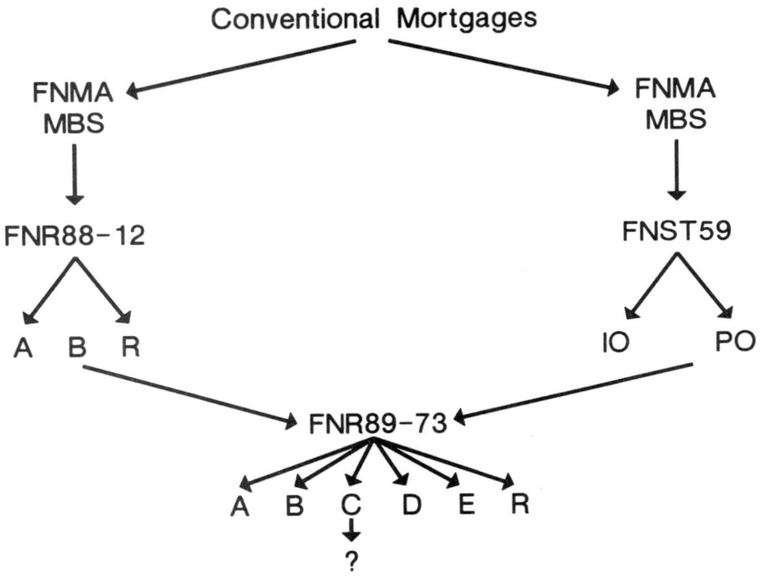

There are several reasons why the increased complexity is less of a problem for most asset-backed securities. One reason is the difference in the absolute quantity of risk. By and large, mortgages have a lot of risk, whereas most asset-backed securities have a relatively small amount of risk. The maturities are shorter, and on those assets where we have prepayment studies, the prepayment variability is also less. Automobile loans, for example, have fairly consistent and predictable prepayments, mostly because it is rarely economical to refinance them. In other cases, such as credit card securities, the security structure insulates the investor from prepayment risks on the collateral.

This leads to the second point, which is that non-mortgage assets are often more problematic than the

Figure 1. CMO Structure

Mae) and put into Fannie Mae mortgage-backed securities. On the left side of the figure is a CMO deal, Fannie Mae REMIC 88-12. On the right side are other mortgages coming out of Fannie Mae and going into the Fannie Mae Strip 59, which has both an interest-only (IO) and a principal-only (PO) piece. The PO strip and the B-tranche from the CMO are both among the collateral put into Fannie Mae REMIC 89-73, which itself has five tranches. There is nothing to prevent any of those tranches from being used as collateral in further deals. This makes it difficult to answer such questions as, "What is the collateral in the deal?" Owen Carney talked about double counting,

resulting asset-backed securities. I often meet somebody from our Asset Finance department wanting to talk about the "optimal" structure for his quarterly pay loans with factors that are three months behind. In these cases, the challenge is to get the assets into *any* security, not to slice them up into 11.3 tranches per deal. If and when such assets are securitized, the security tends to be relatively straightforward compared to the loans themselves.

Finally, there are constraints imposed by issuers.

---

[1]See Mr. Carney's presentation, pp. 66-70.

Mortgage-backed securities effectively do not have an issuer. They are labeled according to who securitizes them—Fannie Mae or Freddie Mac—but these organizations are just securitizers; the ultimate obligors are the homeowners of America. Fannie Mae and Freddie Mac put their seal of approval and guarantee on the securities, but they are not issuers in any conventional sense and they do not look at securities the same way as issuers. They are interested in making fees, so they undertake as much volume as possible with a safe a level of risk.

As a result, there is no limit to how bizarre mortgage-backed securities may get, because it is basically up to the investment banker's imagination. They are trying very hard to solve problems being put forth to them by their customers. They are trying to hone in on specific kinds of risks. The securities that are created can look bizarre, and there is rarely anyone on the other side to argue against them.

This does not happen in asset-backed securities. Asset-backed securities have real issuers—real entities like J.C. Penney, Sears, or Citicorp, that have other issues outstanding in the debt markets and that want their securities to be well understood. These entities carefully consider whether to attach their name to a structure that looks a little odd.

Conclusion

In conclusion, I see the pace of product development abating in the future. Only a few asset classes remain to be securitized in any large quantity. A limited number of foreign capital markets are ready for the technology, and most of them are already players. Complexity in security structure is likely to remain a mortgage market phenomenon and not spread to other asset-backed securities.

Question and Answer Session

Question: How big do you think the asset-backed securities market will be by the end of 1991?

Senft: The market has doubled every year so far, so I think it will double again.

Question: What is your opinion on the lack of portfolio information on automobile and credit card issues in the secondary market? Do you think the lack of information detracts from the liquidity by shrinking the number of potential investors on secondary trading?

Senft: Yes, the lack of information does hurt liquidity. On the other hand, the lack of information is not as bad as it seems. With effort you can get at most of the portfolio data you are interested in. But people want to do stress tests, not just examine the raw data. They want to know at any point in time how much a given security can withstand—how much default rate, how much interest rate movement, and what kind of changes there will be in the average life of the security in each scenario. Not all of this information is easy to get, but it is almost always obtainable. The problem is that these are relatively short-term securities. The spreads are not large, and unless you are talking about a large order, it is difficult to make it worthwhile for investment banks to gather and process all this information. That is precisely the sort of analysis that ought to be done on a joint basis, rather than every dealer having to do it independently.

Question: Given the dramatic widening of spreads on automobile- and credit card-backed securities in the public market, do you think investor confidence in these assets is eroding?

Senft: Maybe I'm wrong, but I really don't think so. In today's capital markets, spreads are widening on most issues and exploding on others. In the capital markets today, I would say the reaction of asset-backed securities is mostly sympathetic to this market movement, with only a small amount the result of specific credit concerns or lack of information. Lack of information hurts liquidity, but it is not the main determiner now in the widening of the spread.

Question: As the asset-backed securities market grows, there will be greater dependence on and desire for a secondary market. What are the prospects for an effective secondary market in the future?

Senft: I define an effective secondary market as one in which you can get a bid or an ask price reasonably quickly, and preferably from more than one investment banker. This situation already exists. It doesn't mean you get the bid that you want, but I don't consider that part of the definition of "effective."

Question: Are you concerned about today's tools for credit enhancement (e.g., letters of credit)? What are the alternatives?

Senft: No, I am not concerned about credit enhancement tools. There are lots of different ways to provide credit enhancement. Issuers tend to drift to the ones that are the most cost-effective at any point in time. Senior/subordinated structures were created because they were cheaper than the alternative methods at the time. In fact, you could make the same statement about virtually any method. When and if confidence in an LOC-type of credit enhancement gets to the point that people (investors, rating agencies, or issuers) just don't want it anymore, then people won't buy it and it will cease to be the cheapest way. They will provide credit enhancement in one of many other ways. So in that sense, I do not see it as a problem.

Self-Evaluation Examination

1. One of the major innovations of asset-backed securities is:
   a. The ability to separate the credit of the asset pool from the underlying credit of an institution.
   b. A reduced need for servicing requirements.
   c. The ability of banks and thrifts to avoid the U.S. Bankruptcy Code.
   d. All of the above.

2. Special-purpose entities created to technically "own" assets in an asset-backed structure can be:
   a. Corporations.
   b. Partnerships.
   c. Trusts.
   d. Any of the above.

3. In securitized transactions, rating agencies:
   a. Play the same role as in the rating of standard corporate debt.
   b. Are more active than in the rating of standard corporate debt.
   c. Play no role because securitized assets do not need ratings given their collateral backing.
   d. Generally look only at the credit rating of the issuing institution.

4. The advent of securitization in the mortgage market has had the following effect on spreads between mortgage rates and U.S. Treasury rates:
   a. Increased spreads.
   b. Decreased spreads.
   c. Had no effect on spreads.
   d. Led to negative spreads.

5. The growth of securitization has led to:
   a. Increased pressures on financial intermediaries whose role has been bypassed in part by products such as securitized mortgages.
   b. Increased spreads between mortgage and U.S. Treasury yields.
   c. Increased ways for institutions to get assets off the balance sheet.
   d. (a) and (b).
   e. (a) and (c).

6. The current policy of the Comptroller about recourse in securitized offerings is best expressed as which one of the following:
   a. The Comptroller is comfortable with FAS 77 and feels that generally accepted accounting principles properly reflect any warranties provided by the seller of securitized products.
   b. The seller can make warranties about activities outside its control to the extent that such warranties are deemed prudent by FAS 77.
   c. The Comptroller wants warranties by the seller to be limited to those activities under the seller's control.
   d. Warranties by the seller are properly priced in the market, and hence, are not of concern to the Comptroller.

7. Which of the following is *not* an obstacle to increased complexity (i.e., many complicated tranches) in asset-backed securities as compared to mortgage-backed securities:
   a. Most securitized assets generally have less risk than mortgages and, hence, not as complex a structure is needed to parcel out the risk.

    b.   Although mortgage-backed securities do not have a true issuer (other than a collection of homeowners), many asset-backed securities involve identities of real entities (major corporations) who hesitate lending their name to very complicated tranches.

    c.   Compared to mortgages, many assets being securitized have longer maturities, which lead to simpler structures.

8.   The following countries are where the chief issuers of mortgage- or asset-backed securities have been as of late 1990:

    a.   United States, United Kingdom, Canada, Australia, and France.
    b.   United States, United Kingdom, Germany, Japan, and Holland.
    c.   United States, United Kingdom, and Japan.
    d.   United States, Germany, and Japan.

9.   What are the two direct benefits a bank obtains from securitizing a portion of its production?

10.   The cost of bank lending is the marginal cost of its certificates of deposit.

    a.   True.
    b.   False.

11.   Banks with a strong local presence have an advantage in securitization.

    a.   True.
    b.   False.

12.   Credit monitoring tends to be irrelevant in securitization.

    a.   True.
    b.   False.

13.   Bank analysts have a tougher time doing their jobs today because:

    a.   Securitized assets do not appear anywhere in the financial statements.
    b.   Income from securitization is reported differently than other noninterest income.
    c.   Banks do not report the results of securitization.
    d.   None of the above.

14.   Securitization has value for bank rearrangement because it can help: (1) spread risks; (2) balance interest rate risk; (3) increase income; (4) enhance liquidity.

    a.   (1) only.
    b.   (1) and (3).
    c.   (2) and (4).
    d.   All of the above.

15.   What is rebound risk? (1) The risk that the asset securitized and sold will be the liability of the bank. (2) The risk that income from securitized assets will be less than expected. (3) The risk that buyers of securitized assets will default.

    a.   (1) only.
    b.   (2) only.
    c.   (3) only.
    d.   (1) and (2).

16.   The Resolution Trust Corporation (RTC) has had no effect on the market for securitized assets.

    a.   True.
    b.   False.

17.   Portfolio managers will not be affected by the FIRREA risk-rate rule changes.

    a.   True.
    b.   False.

18. What sorts of assets lend themselves to securitization?
    a. Accounts receivable.
    b. Inventories.
    c. Commercial mortgages.
    d. Franchise payments.
    e. Stable cash flows from business units.
    f. All the above.
    g. None of the above.

19. U.S. debt interest expenses may be used fully to offset income from international operations.
    a. True.
    b. False.

20. An investors's exposure to event risk may be partially mitigated by purchasing a company's securitized debt rather than the company's debt itself.
    a. True.
    b. False.

21. Which of the following attributes is *least* descriptive of a CMO?
    a. More liquid than a mortgage-backed security.
    b. Competes more directly with corporate and Treasury bonds than does a mortgage-backed security.
    c. Reallocates the total mortgage-backed security risk across tranches.
    d. At issuance the value of the CMO pieces exceeds its collateral.

22. When valuing CMOs, which of the following tactics is *least* likely to succeed?
    a. Measure CMO risk by computing the contribution to portfolio risk.
    b. Choose the highest option-adjusted spread securities.
    c. Dissect each security into simpler pieces to evaluate.
    d. Reconstruct cash flows under various prepayment assumptions.

23. The option-adjusted spread is
    a. A negative spread over Treasuries.
    b. Independent of the simulation method used for pricing.
    c. A reconciliation between simulation price and the actual market value of a mortgage-backed security.
    d. Constant across all tranches of a CMO.

24. Simulation is an important tool when analyzing mortgage-backed securities because
    a. The expected cash flows are dependent on the cash flows actually paid in the past.
    b. The structure of the CMO's high-risk tranches depends on the cash flows made to the more senior tranches.
    c. The rate paid by adjustable-rate mortgages depends on the path of past interest rates.
    d. All of the above.

25. The principal advantage of using asset-backed securities rather than mortgage-backed securities in an arbitrage position is
    a. Shorter expected average life.
    b. More stable and predictable cash flows.
    c. Wider spreads for similar risk.
    d. Ability to synthetically realize relative value between fixed- and floating-rate markets.
    e. All of the above.

26. For a successful asset-backed securities and swap transaction, which of the following is not important?
    a.   Predictable cash flows to avoid over- or under-swapped positions.
    b.   Flat term structure.
    c.   Liquid markets for swaps and asset-backed securities.
    d.   Ability to realize yields equal to or greater than targeted.
    e.   Creditworthy swap counterparties and asset-backed securities issuers.

Self-Evaluation Answers

1. a. According to Peters, if structured properly an asset-backed security will not be encumbered by provisions of the U.S. Bankruptcy Code.

2. d. See Peters.

3. b. According to Peters, rating agencies typically analyze the servicer, collateral, cash flow structure, and remoteness of the security to bankruptcy, as well as other factors.

4. b. According to BeVier, the increased efficiency in the market resulting from marketable mortgage-backed securities has made it cheaper for the ultimate homeowner to borrow funds.

5. e. According to BeVier, securitization bypasses some of the traditional intermediation functions of thrifts and banks. The resultant decreases in spreads between mortgages and U.S. Treasuries has put extra pressures on financial institutions. At the same time, securitization gives financial institutions a way to remove assets (e.g., mortgages) from their balance sheets.

6. c. See Carney.

7. c. According to Senft, both (a) and (b) are reasons that asset-backed securities are not likely to be as complex as mortgage-backed securities.

8. a. See Senft.

9.   See Ocampo. The two benefits are (1) improved capital efficiency and (2) deposit repricing.

10. b. See Ocampo. False. The bank cannot price-discriminate. Thus, the actual cost depends on the average CD price and the cannibalization impact on the lower-priced deposits.

11. a. See Ocampo. True. They have an advantage because they can tap scale economies.

12. b. See Ocampo. False. It is very important to eventual loss results.

13. b. See Welsh. Banks report securitized asset income in other noninterest income.

14. c. See Welsh.

15. d. See Welsh.

16. b. See Bortel. False. It affects the confidence of the Congress and security buyers.

17. b. See Bortel. False. The risk-weighted capital rule change will injure the attraction of this enhancer.

18. f. See Wigdortz.

19. b. See Wigdortz. False. Interest allocation rules prevent using all of the interest expense in U.S. debt to offset income from foreign operations.

20. a. The assets backing the debt may be of a different credit, and represent the risk of the asset rather than the issuer.

21. a. Dunn points out that a CMO actually loses liquidity relative to the mortgage-backed security. The reallocation of risk is the primary advantage of the CMO.

22. b. Dunn warns that the option-adjusted spread can be very misleading and gives an example to illustrate the point.

23. c. Richard defines option-adjusted spread as the increment to the Treasury yield that equates simulation value to the observed price.

24. d. See Richard.

25. e. See Dillon.

26. b. See Dillon's section on "Requirements for Successful Asset-Backed Securities/Swap Transactions."